DEEP TRUTH

Deep Truth

Jacob Einholt Himmelman

To order additional copies of this book, contact:
Xlibris Corporation
1-888-795-4274
www.Xlibris.com
Orders@Xlibris.com
43353

CONTENTS

DEDICATION

This book is dedicated to the development of humanity.

ABOUT THE AUTHOR

Hello to all my readers. We meet through the medium of the written word. I am a research scientist. Those of us in this group are in-depth analysts in all matters. Thus, this work is not just a compilation of facts and dates; it contains my analysis of American problems with solutions to the problems.

In scientific matters, research scientists are often considered to have strange ideas since we usually work within areas at the front edge of science. This usually creates a lonely life and, in truth, helps the researcher to concentrate on his or her work. As you read my several publications, you will know that my reclusive, pensive nature enabled me to merge my mortal mind with a higher consciousness. Without being aware of a change of consciousness, I thought that I was discovering great secrets of the universe. In truth, through my mortal mind, new knowledge was being brought into the world from the higher consciousness.

As a research scientist, my studies into science and the affairs of humanity is reveals,the truth, and often-scathing truth. However, when comparisons are made to statements made by Washington officials, the language used in this historic review is mild. For example: President Truman's response to Drew Pearson saying, "What the president should have done," was, "No son of a bitch news reporter is going to tell me what to do," and President Kennedy's scathing comment when steelmakers raised the price of steel—"My father always told me that businessmen were sons of bitches." Senator Bob Dole used similar insulting language with me via the phone one morning, probably from the office of Manus Cooney, after I faxed an apropos blunt letter about the wrong decision to send American troops to Bosnia. Senator Bob Dole said to me, "Jack, you are a ruthless son of a bitch." Also, the remark that Lyndon B. Johnson made in reference to the people of the *New York Times* should not be forgotten. Lyndon B. Johnson said of the *New York Times*'s people, they are a "bunch of commies," meaning communists.

Also, the work of Michael Isikoff and David Corn, culminating in the book *Hubris,* was most revealing about President Bush's outburst to Ari Fleischer. His coarse language to Ari Fleischer when Ari told President Bush about Helen

Thomas's questions about a looming war, also revealed his intent to invade Iraq. President Bush said to Ari: "Did you tell her I'm going to kick his sorry motherfuc—ass all over the Mideast?"

Therefore, in consideration of the blunt language used by elected officials in Washington, I should be granted the right to state in blunt terms the nature of Congress members and presidents according to my analysis.

A DESIRE TO AVOID GREAT FANFARE

Many writers wish to protect their privacy and use a pseudonym with some of their work. With this publication, this is my situation, for my true name is not Jacob Einholt Himmelman. However, Jacob is my first name in German.

A three-volume work will follow this publication, and my true name will be revealed. However, if any member of the federal government wishes to make contact with me, my publisher will accommodate their request.

The historical data for this book comes from many sources, including the *New York Times*, *Wall Street Journal*, *San Francisco Chronicle*, Knight Ridder publications, *Washington Post*, tapping the voluminous data from Google, Fox News, and historical data recorded in the books of Michael Isikoff, David Corn, and Bob Woodward. No literary works are plagiarized. Only the historical data was used as to when and where something happened and who the participants in the historic events were.

CHAPTER ONE

A NEW BIRTH OF FREEDOM
AND WEALTH

Americans are on the verge of receiving greater freedom and wealth than they ever before experienced. How this wealth will be distributed is explained carefully in this book.

The reason why America was attacked is also explained in this book. While the scars and trauma from the 9/11 attacks will linger for a while, this bad memory will slowly fade into history.

Americans must become ready to receive a great gift that will alter lifestyles forever.

NEW BLESSINGS ARE COMING THAT CAN NEVER BE TAKEN AWAY.

Books from this first publication may become a collector's item in the future because the knowledge in this book will change the world. People in the civilized hi-tech nations will receive the greatest blessings. These people are interested in inventions that will improve their lifestyle. They know that blessings come from harnessing the environment and creating systems that enable free people to enjoy a higher standard of living. Therefore, the people of all industrialized nations will be interested in this book, for they are on the verge of a new birth of freedom and wealth.

Some changes must be made to enable a new life to become reality. Although, the new life will not come automatically, for there are several changes that must be made to enable Americans to enjoy more freedom and wealth. However, America put men on the moon, so making changes to adapt to the new freedom and wealth will be easy.

America needs millions of gallons of gasoline and diesel fuel each day to power automobiles. Paying thirty, forty, and fifty dollars to fill up the fuel tank each week can soon be forever gone. The fruits from the labors of inventors in industrialized nations are about to free their nations from an oil cartel that was formed to fix prices and manipulate the supply of oil. Hydrogen is the fuel that will replace gasoline and diesel fuel. A new discovery in the process of extracting hydrogen from water will make hydrogen less expensive than any fossil fuel.

IN THE PAST, DUE TO THE SHORTAGE OF GASOLINE, VIOLENCE ERUPTED FROM LONG LINES AT THE GAS PUMP. IN RESPONSE TO OIL PRICES AND SHORTAGES, PEOPLE IN POWERFUL POSITIONS CONSIDERED VIOLENCE AS A WAY TO SOLVE THIS PROBLEM.

During the Clinton administration, some powerful people of huge corporations that were victims of the oil cartel's economic warfare became distraught from the financial burden, and instead of using brains to defeat the oil cartel, some considered using brawn, or warfare, to solve the problem. It was a bad idea.

AN INVASION OF ARABIA WAS REPORTED TO HAVE BEEN DISCUSSED IN WASHINGTON DURING THE CLINTON ADMINISTRATION.

American oil companies have not forgotten how the Saudis confiscated their Arabian oil wells in a political maneuver by the Saudis called nationalization. These same oil companies have lobbyists and powerful friends in Washington. Whether these powerful oil company people were behind a plot to use war to take back their once-owned oil wells might be discovered by an independent congressional investigation. Although don't put any hopes in that happening, for sleazy politicians ignored the facts about Bill Clinton's lies and certainly would not go after any "buccaneering capitalists."

AN INSIDIOUS PLOT WAS REVEALED BY THE
WALL STREET JOURNAL

On February 4, 2004, the *Wall Street Journal* emblazoned their front page with a revelation, or an accusation, about the war hawks in Washington planning to invade Arabia to get their oil fields. That was 1996, and thankfully it didn't happen.

However, the respected *Wall Street Journal* does not use their front page to print rumors. The reporter probably had a reliable "deep throat" informer, or it wouldn't have printed the article. Assuming the article had a basis of truth, it revealed the deceptive, lying political gangsters in the federal government and maybe powerful "buccaneering capitalists" that were working behind the scenes.

In order to invade Arabia, the American public would have had to have been primed to believe it was right and necessary to invade Arabia. Lies and deception are the modus operandi of the Washington "political gangsters." Just as Truman used his "police action" lies to gain public support for his Korean "Caesar" exploit, Bill Clinton's "I didn't have sex with that girl" lies, and George W. Bush justified a "Caesar" exploit, invading Iraq to have himself glorified as a great commander-in-chief.

WHY 9/11 RESEARCHERS NEED TO DIG DEEPER FOR THE REASONS

A terrible attractive force was generated in the American psyche to balance the Law of Recompense or "as ye sow so shall ye reap" principle. To what degree the plan to invade Arabia helped bring about or had an effect on the 9/11 attack, we cannot know from normal means.

It has been rumored or intentionally leaked that the Saudis became aware of Washington's plan to invade their country and to destroy their oil wells. This terrible idea was not taken lightly by the Muslim nation of Arabia. It is doubtful that we can ever know, by normal means, how much retaliation Arabian Muslims planned. The fact that fifteen of the nineteen kamikaze terrorists that downed the Twin Towers were Arabians seems to be more than coincidental.

One fact stands out as bright as the noonday sun on a clear day. As the knowledge spread in the Muslim hierarchy about a planned attack on Mohammed's birthplace and the center of the Islamic faith, retaliation was planned, for an attack on Arabia would be understood as an attack on all Muslim people.

Mid-Eastern oil-producing nations know that oil and its products grease and power the machinery of the mechanized world. Industrialized nations and especially America have been and are financially squeezed by OPEC since Arabia has created a cartel and fixes prices. It is no wonder that some greedy and powerful men in Washington wanted to invade Arabia.

OIL-RICH NATIONS HAVE ALSO USED THEIR ACQUIRED CAPITAL NOT ONLY TO WAGE AN ECONOMIC WAR, A STATE OF DECLARED WAR IS CARRIED OUT BY EXTREMISTS IN THE FORM OF TERRORIST ACTS AGAINST CHRISTIAN, JEWISH, AND HINDU NATIONS.

Unfortunately for the people of the United States, Congress has not declared a state of war on terrorism. This would eliminate any elected politician from using their office to operate as a self-styled "Caesar."

Caesars, whether self-styled or reigning as an emperor, could not operate without the support of the legislative body and campaign dollars. Serving "special interest groups" has been and is the means to raise capital for the costs of reelection campaigns.

Most abuses against the vast majority have come from more-than-one-term politicians. Therefore, for the interest of the vast majority, it is necessary to establish one-term limits for federal offices. The length of service has been wisely suggested to be eight years for members of the Senate and four years for members of the House of Representatives. This constitutional change must come in order to protect and expand America's freedom and wealth.

However, this is only one political change that is necessary. Another change that is far more powerful for the increase of freedom and wealth for all Americans is to radically change the structure of the economic system by eliminating our dependence on oil as an energy source. Keep reading, for the reading material will become astonishing to you.

HYDROGEN IS THE INEXHAUSTIBLE SOURCE OF ENERGY THAT CAN REPLACE ALL FOSSIL FUELS AND CAN BE HAD FOR A FRACTION OF THE COST OF GASOLINE AND DIESEL FUEL.

Petroleum, coal, and natural gas cannot continue to be the world's chief sources of energy. In time, each will become scarcer and more expensive to retrieve from Mother Earth. Reserves of crude oil and natural gas will be depleted in fifty years.

Waste-to-energy plants, wind-driven turbines, solar panels, and geothermal plants are necessary to alleviate the demand for fossil fuels and protect the environment. In addition, thermal polymerization (renamed thermal conversion) can have a niche in "waste to energy" applications. However, there is not enough waste to polymerize into oil to replace all the petroleum products needed. Another aspect about thermal conversion is the fact that it may be too expensive to be a viable option for creating oil from wastes.

Ethanol from corn and sugarcane and gasoline from coal are also more expensive than gasoline from crude oil and therefore can only alleviate the heavy demand for petroleum products. Only if acres of solar panels or a geothermal plant could supply electricity would processing plants to process corn into ethanol be cost-competitive. However, ethanol is not as good as gasoline and hydrogen as a fuel for internal combustion engines; it has a lower explosive power and is slightly corrosive. In addition, using vast quantities of corn to make ethanol sends profits to a "special interest group" and fuels the forces of inflation. Using corn to make ethanol has already made corn more expensive for human food. In addition, cereals, milk, bread, eggs, plus meat from poultry, pork, and beef, whose food stock uses corn, has also increased in price. It is a case of political hypocrisy that while government officials claim to be against inflation, their financing the programs to make ethanol from corn actually is an inflation engine. Unfortunately for millions of the poor and middle class, they pay a greater dollar share from this engineered inflation.

The price increases related to using corn to make ethanol ares unnecessary, and the direct blame cannot be averted; they are due to the federal government policies. Instead of using corn to make ethanol, the oil-rich seedpods from the jatropha (ya-tr-fa) plant are far better than corn to make biofuels, and it is the best agricultural plant on the planet to make biofuel. Since jatropha is inedible, its use for a biofuel has no inflationary effect on food products. In addition, the cost to produce biofuel from the jatropha plant is about half the cost of corn-based ethanol and one third the cost of rapeseed.

To learn more about this biofuel miracle plant, go to Google and type *jatropha*.

Biofuel from this plant can be used to alleviate the crunch that is occurring from dwindling fossil fuels. Science's leading advisors have been warning the world for several decades concerning the dwindling fossil fuel reserves. The world depending upon fossil fuel as an energy source will cause energy costs to escalate over long time periods, said many prophetic scientists, and their predictions have come true. Yet only when the world felt the energy crunch and the pinch from the oil cartel in 1978, 1979, 1980, and 2006 were programs established to seek relief, and since then, millions of dollars have been spent on research, publications, and funding for new enterprises that might provide alternate energy sources. Yet the demand for crude oil has increased with the growing Asian needs.

SCIENCE'S LEADING MENTORS HAVE STATED REPEATEDLY: The world needs more electricity to be supplied by atomic power plants operated by the FUSION technique, and the world needs an inexpensive method to extract HYDROGEN from water.

FUSION techniques are being advanced, and the timetable for fusion to become commercially practical is within a timetable that has been continually one to two decades away, like a carrot on a stick in front of a walking horse. The decade and a half away continually moves away as time passes. IF and that is a big IF, FUSION ever does replace FISSION as the atomic technique, environmental contamination will be eliminated, gone will be possible meltdowns, radioactive leaks into the environment, and great hazards from radioactive waste products. However, the technology to harness hydrogen's FUSION power is tremendously expensive and may be impractical, while HYDROGEN is readily available.

Scientists have made great discoveries in their search to extract hydrogen from water in commercial quantities. However, the discoveries are only for laboratory demonstrations. Among the discoveries are fuel cells, new types of membranes, and "Vulcan Chemistry." All are fascinating to see and ponder about, yet only "Vulcan chemistry" has yielded any promising techniques in the search for profitably extracting hydrogen from water.

Germany and Japan, followed by Switzerland and Israel, are leading the world in hydrogen research and the new aspect, "Vulcan Chemistry." However, there is a barrier since electrolysis requires electricity, and electricity is not free.

This factor has not enabled scientists to make hydrogen commercially available at a low cost.

However, Iceland, with its free geothermal energy resource, has been able to make hydrogen less expensive than petroleum fuels.

ICELAND USES HEAT FROM A GEOTHERMAL SOURCE. AT THE PRESENT, FREE HEAT OR FREE ELECTRICAL ENERGY TO ELECTROLYZE WATER CAN MAKE HYDROGEN LESS EXPENSIVE THAN FOSSIL FUELS.

Although, even without the resource of geothermal heat, heating water to "superheated status" has enabled scientists to extract hydrogen from vapor in quantities unprecedented in the history of electrolysis. However, the quanta of energy spent to heat the water (not including the cost of the expensive apparatus) only raised their formula to a higher level.

WITH SUPERHEATED WATER, there are greater quanta of energy being extracted in the form of hydrogen. However, on the other side of the equation, without free energy from a geothermal source, there is even more energy being spent to heat the water for extracting the hydrogen.

UNTIL MY DISCOVERY, NO ONE HAS YET BEEN ABLE TO CIRCUMVENT (or get around) FARADAY'S LAW. HIS LAW IS A SCIENTIFIC PRINCIPLE. SIMPLY STATED, IT IS: YOU CANNOT GET SOMETHING FOR NOTHING.

THE LAW OF CONSERVATION OF ENERGY, i.e., ENERGY CANNOT BE CREATED, STANDS RESOLUTE.

However, I have discovered that a certain catalyst, when used with a new electrolyte in an electrolyzer, DOES enable greater quantities of water to be separated into hydrogen and oxygen.

Therefore, my discovery of an inexpensive catalyst that enables the electrolysis process to be raised to a higher level is made possible by the fact that the electrolysis process harnesses the energy impacted in the catalyst.

Therefore, HYDROGEN as a source of energy IS available NOW and IS inexhaustible. Are you ready to "gas up" with hydrogen? Only by public pressure upon Congress can hydrogen become the miracle fuel of the future.

The amount of energy in the form of hydrogen taken from a gallon of water is about equal to how far an automobile will travel on a gallon of gasoline.

In addition, hydrogen as a fuel for internal combustion engines and turbines is superior to a petroleum fuel for two reasons. First and foremost, there is no pollution. The only exhaust coming from the exhaust pipe is water vapor. Secondly, hydrogen's power can be illustrated by comparing it to the octane rating of 93 for gasoline, for hydrogen on the same comparison would have the octane rating of about 112 to 115. Hydrogen as a fuel for internal combustion engines is about 25 percent more efficient than gasoline. Also, in comparison to natural gas, hydrogen contains three times the energy, pound for pound, as natural gas.

For those that want more information about hydrogen, it is available on the Web. However, you will not find any information about the miracle that I have discovered.

SWITCHING GASOLINE AND DIESEL-POWERED ENGINES TO USE HYDROGEN FUEL WILL NOT BE A PROBLEM.

Many manufactures of internal combustion engines already have engines fitted for the use of a gaseous fuel. Some American engines are powered by propane, pure natural gas, and some are powered by HYDROGEN.

GM unveiled a hydrogen-powered car in January 2005 named the Sequel; it uses compressed hydrogen. Eight kilograms of compressed hydrogen can power the Sequel for three hundred miles. That prototype portends the future for automobiles, and it cannot come too soon. Using hydrogen to power automobiles is near, but to get it in the marketplace, you, as a member of the public, must pressure Congress.

Also, the Germans have developed an engine that uses either gasoline or hydrogen. Although the Germans store hydrogen by supercooling, this method is expensive and is not as desirable as storing hydrogen in pressurized tanks. Hydride tanks are another method to store hydrogen although, at the present state of the art, they are too heavy to be practicable. Research is ongoing to make hydrides more efficient. The company that makes solar cell roofing material that is headed by Stanford R. Ovshinsky is working on a new hydride for storing hydrogen.

A DISTRIBUTION SYSTEM FOR HYDROGEN IS NEEDED

A serious hydrogen program to begin switching to hydrogen on a national scale will require time. More than a decade will be needed to switch most of the gas and diesel stations to hydrogen, for there are about 170,000 retail gas stations in America. However, the greatest percentage of gasoline is used in the Eastern United States. Therefore, hydrogen stations would naturally be built in LA and other large cities on the West Coast and in America's largest East Coast cities. Until the American economy becomes hydrogen-powered, biofuel from the jatropha plant could help to make America energy independent.

TRANSPORTING HYDROGEN

In the cases where huge electrolyzers cannot be built at the gas stations, hydrogen can be transported to gas stations by tanker, just as gasoline is today.

In addition to the tanker method, the most efficient method would be to transport hydrogen by pipeline. At the present, in America, there are only about seven hundred miles of pipeline to transport hydrogen. These are used by oil refineries to process crude oil.

However, the French do have one 250-mile pipeline, between France and Belgium, for transporting hydrogen to a petroleum refinery. However, when hydrogen is transported by pipeline, it tends to make metal pipes brittle and prone to cracking. Therefore, pipes must be coated with a plastic that protects the metal. This would cost an enormous amount of money. However, the Iraq war already cost about five hundred billion (including over 3,000 American deaths), and the war may cost a trillion dollars (and 5,000 deaths), with NO gain for America.

HYDROGEN HAS BEEN CALLED THE PERFECT FUEL. NUCLEAR POWER PLANTS WILL BE REPLACED BY HYDROGEN POWERED TURBINES.

Fission to produce steam for turbines was touted as one of the greatest blessings to humanity. Instead it has become one of mankind's greatest curses. The use of hydrogen for power plants will bring an end to radioactive waste from nuclear power plants. Also, it will prevent any accidents such as Three Mile Island, Chernobyl, and nuclear-powered submarines being scuttled or accidentally sinking to the bottom of the ocean.

THE USE OF HYDROGEN WAS PREDICTED IN JULES VERN'S SCIENCE NOVELS.

The last and long-awaited prediction of Jules Vern has come true. In one novel of Jules Verne, written on 1874, titled *The Mysterious Island*, the world travelers came upon an island where all their energy needs was taken from water. Iceland is not mysterious; however, it is the first island to use hydrogen—taken from water—to power a few internal combustion engines. However, Japan is more technically savvy and business oriented than Iceland, and these conditions make Japan the logical choice to become the world's first hydrogen-powered economy.

COMMERCIAL-SIZE ELECTROLYZERS WILL BE HUGE

Building a commercial-size electrolyzer has been and is beyond my personal financial ability. Also, applying for patents myself for such a world-changing device would be as foolish as a prospector going into a bar during the California Gold Rush and shouting, "I found it! I found an El Dorado," then stating, "I know that I can trust you fellows," proceeding to draw a map to where he found the gold.

As a research scientist, I have longed to bring my discovery to the marketplace. However, only companies that already have a distribution system for natural gas, gasoline, and diesel fuel would be the most logical candidates to become the chief stations to sell hydrogen. Therefore, I tried to interest certain companies in the extraction and distribution of hydrogen—to no avail. I tried to interest some venture capitalists without success. I made a trip to the Japanese embassy in Washington in hopes of interesting Japanese companies to be the lead companies that would free their nation from being another hostage to the oil cartel. I never received a letter from the embassy officer.

I then decided to write President Bush a letter about my electrolysis discovery. Following is a copy of that letter:

> President Bush: President Roosevelt received the most important letter that he ever received from a civilian that was dated August 2, 1939. This letter informed President Roosevelt that a SUPER BOMB could be built. The letter that originated from Princeton University was conceived by Dr. Leo Szilard and Dr. Edward Teller and was actually written by Dr. Leo Szilard. These two physicists decided to use the prestige and reputation of Dr. Albert Einstein to get the attention of President Roosevelt. Dr. Leo Szilard explained to Einstein the method to create chain reaction fission and therefore a SUPER BOMB. Einstein was convinced and remarked, "I never thought of that" and agreed to sign his name to a letter that Dr. Szilard would write. That was 1939 and nothing could be done at that time, but shortly after Pearl Harbor was attacked, the Manhattan Project was funded, and the project to build an ATOMIC BOMB began.
>
> Now history is repeating, for this letter will be the most important letter you will ever receive from a civilian.
>
> Since our country and most of the industrialized world is dependent upon oil from Arab nations, our nation's foreign policy is shaped by this fact. This dependency reduces our options in dealing with "war crazed" tyrants and Muslim nations that hatch and harbor Muslim terrorists.
>
> The "silver bullet" or solution to this dilemma is being presented to you in this letter. Please read the next few lines carefully.
>
> Hydrogen is the next and inexhaustible energy source that will replace gasoline, diesel fuel, and home heating oil.
>
> Mr. President: I know how to build electrolyzers that will extract hydrogen from water in vast quantities that will make hydrogen less expensive that any fossil fuel.
>
> I have not tried to patent this process for obvious reasons if you are savvy about patent infringement, for not only would I receive about

as much as Sutter received from the squatters that took gold from his land, but the great frenzy to extract hydrogen, store it, and distribute it by multi-billion dollar oil companies would relegate me to being almost a non-entity. I know they would claim to be honest and clamor "take us to court."

Mr. President: It required years for Dr. Land to get a settlement from Kodak for patent infringement and other patent infringement cases also have taken years.

Therefore, Mr. President, just as Dr. Leo Szilard's letter required special consideration, this letter requires special consideration. I propose a plan that will make America energy free and the first leader in exporting hydrogen. I state the first leader because once other industrialized nations are knowledgeable about the process; they will establish their own hydrogen industry.

The key factor in switching to hydrogen as a fuel source is making it available for millions of automobiles, trucks, and other vehicles that use a crude oil derived fuel. Therefore, present oil companies will be the future hydrogen industry.

I know my knowledge is also a multi-billion dollar idea, and I am sure that big oil companies would be in capitalistic ecstasy, if I would simply freely explain how to build the electrolyzers. But, sir, inventors do have a right to be rewarded for their intellectual property. Therefore, sir, you and Vice President Dick Cheney have the contacts to interest a big oil company in buying my intellectual property.

I know hydrogen has now become strategically important to America, and I also know that you can arrange a meeting of oil executives and myself to work out fair compensation for my intellectual property."

My letter was never answered.

Then, on August 21, 2004, I wrote a letter to Senator Charles Schumer of New York. I then wrote a letter on October 11, 2004, to the governor of California, Arnold Schwarzenegger. These letters were also never answered. However, in a ploy to give appearances of doing something about the energy problem, President Bush and Vice President Cheney informed the public that an energy crisis meeting would be held at the White House. Vice President Cheney chaired the meeting, and old friends of President Bush and VP Cheney from ENRON—yes, ENRON—plus other oil companies were present. BUT no one was present from the wind power industry, the waste-to-energy industry, the geothermal industry (Calpine), or someone knowledgeable about hydrogen. That suggests that the Bush and Cheney interest in the petroleum industry was paramount for their good even into a long-range energy program. It is evident that protecting their own interest is more important than the interests of the American people.

After not receiving an answer to the letter informing President Bush about hydrogen as a new energy source, I wrote a second letter. It follows:

May 1, 2006

President George W. Bush
White House
Washington D.C.

Fax reading employee:
If you want to do one task right—in your lifetime, MAKE SURE THE PRESIDENT GETS THIS FAX MESSAGE.

Mr. President:
I wrote to you before about a means and method to extract HYDROGEN from water that would make the price of an equivalent amount of hydrogen to a gallon of gasoline between 25 to 50 cents.

You did not respond. Dick Cheney is not interested in an innovative method to solve the world's energy crisis. He believes—let industry in a laissez-faire mode allow market forces to bring hydrogen to general usage. Big laugh—when they are making billions and don't want to upset their status quo.

I need to know if this message is being ignored, or do you want to know HOW to establish a HYDROGEN INDUSTRY—or don't you want to know?

I've sent a fax letter before about my knowledge HOW to build a new type electrolyzer. Are you interested?

I need to know the answers to these questions in order to include your response in a book that I am writing.

I received no answer to this letter.

ENERGY CRISIS ADDRESSED

In President Bush's January 28, 2003, State of the Union address, he devoted the following four paragraphs to America's energy problem.

Tonight, I'm proposing $1.2 billion in research funding so that America can lead the world in developing clean, hydrogen-powered automobiles.

A simple chemical reaction between hydrogen and oxygen generates energy, which can be used to power a car, producing only water, not exhaust fumes. With a new national commitment, our scientists and engineers will overcome obstacles to taking these cars from laboratory to showroom, so that the first car driven by a child born today could be powered by hydrogen, and pollution-free. Join me in this important innovation to make our air significantly cleaner, and our country much less dependent on foreign sources of energy.

President Bush's reference to membrane technology in the second paragraph is the basis for the four paragraphs. It is a fantasy, for this process cannot power an automobile.

However, fuel cells were once the hope for electricity to power an electric motor and hybrid automobiles. The fuel cell was invented in 1839, and since then, it has remained a source for special applications. However, the Honda Corporation, through intense research, has raised the fuel cell to high efficiency. At the present, their fuel cell for automobiles is 20 percent smaller, 30 percent lighter, and the power output has been increased to 100 kilowatts. In addition, Japan's Hitachi Company is experimenting with a ruthenium-based catalyst that could raise the efficiency of fuel cells.

Although the price of an automobile with fuel cell power is still beyond the means of the vast middle class, automobiles that run on compressed hydrogen are already available at no extra cost.

Later in 2006, President Bush stated to Congress that America was addicted to foreign oil. Most eighth-grade students are aware of that fact. However, no plan to greatly reduce our oil imports was introduced.

NEW OIL FIELDS IN ALASKA SHOULD NOT BE THE FIRST OPTION.

According to the Energy Information Administration, when President Bush gave the 2006 address to Congress, America was consuming more than twenty million barrels of oil per day. Of that amount, over eleven million barrels were imported.

President Bush could have submitted an "American Energy Act" that would have substantially reduced America's need for foreign oil.

Simply by mandating all first-, second-, and third-class cities to have a waste-to-energy plant or plants sufficient to burn all their garbage or lose grants of federal government money would have enabled a great reduction of imported oil.

New York City and surrounding densely populated regions need electric power while New York City does not even have an incinerator to generate electricity. Their garbage is a valuable resource that could be used to generate electricity, but instead, some of their garbage is shipped hundreds of miles away, even to Virginia and the York County incinerator that is located in the county where I live. It costs New York City $400 million a year to ship their garbage when plasma gasification plants could reverse their expenses to a profitable cash inflow.

INCINERATOR REPORT

A report for the year 2002 for the York, Pennsylvania, and incinerator plant was published on the net. The data follows. The population of York County in 2002 was about 250,000 people. That is a quarter of a million people, while New York City had a population of 8.3 MILLION people. The York, Pennsylvania, incinerator report revealed great news for turning garbage into electricity. The number of gross kilowatt-hours of electricity generated in 2002 was 264,556,000. That saved 552,000 barrels of oil that did not have to be imported from Muslim OPEC. The amount of electricity generated and sold to GPU (General Public Utilities) was enough to provide the energy for 20,000 to 30,000 homes. In addition, 114,840 tons of ash recycled into aggregate was used for construction projects.

Therefore, New York City, with 8.4 million people, has sixteen times more people than York County.

With more waste-to-energy plants in operation, the demand for imported petroleum from Arab nations could be substantially reduced.

More electrical generating plants using geothermal technology, used tires, plasma gasification plants that convert waste to useful products and electricity, and conventional waste-to-energy plants need to be built.

All waste-to-energy plants should be legally mandated to produce hydrogen when the demand for electricity and steam is less than its capacity.

All electrical generation plants should be legally mandated to produce hydrogen on "off peak" hours, instead of "shutting down" a portion of its generating capacity.

These electrical generating plants should be the only government-franchised independent producers of hydrogen.

In addition, a greater use of natural gas to power some electrical generating plants would use home-owned natural gas instead of imported oil. Also, the electricity generated could power electric "mailsters" for the postal service in metropolitan areas.

Switching all postal service mailsters in densely populated regions to electric-powered vehicles would save tens of thousands of barrels of imported oil. In addition, every federal and state government vehicle (excluding military) could be fitted to run on natural gas where natural gas is available. Lastly, a careful study should have been made of all electrical appliances to determine if they are as energy efficient as they could be. Implementing these seven ideas would save millions of barrels of oil a year.

PRESIDENT BUSH FAILED TO ADVANCE THESE ENERGY-SAVING IDEAS.

Some of these real petroleum-saving ideas that could be implemented on a national level are not new. They have been suggested and never implemented. These energy-saving ideas could reduce the amount of crude imported from the oil cartel and bring down the price of gasoline at the pump. It would not be a panacea for America's energy crisis, for internal combustion engines consume two thirds of American oil consumption. However, considering the deficit in trade and the high prices for energy, these energy-saving ideas should have been implemented long ago.

MORE TIME WAS GIVEN TO ME TO MEDITATE ABOUT THE VAST BLESSINGS OF A NATIONAL HYDROGEN INDUSTRY.

At this time in my life, being near eighty years old, the following reoccurring thought kept coming to my mind: if I did become a multimillionaire, how could I best use the money to advance mankind. From this meditation, a new and marvelous idea came to me. I would give the profits, which would ordinarily be allotted to me, to the American public. After arriving at this possibility, several ideas came to my mind. I eventually settled on an idea that would bring a new freedom and wealth to 90 percent of the American people. I would give what would be my profits to a Social Security Fund.

The reason I state 90 percent of the American people would benefit is because 10 percent of Americans have sufficient wealth to live with a high standard of living. Powering the cars with hydrogen for this upper 10 percent would do little to change their standard of living.

NEW LAWS MUST BE WRITTEN. A NATIONAL REFERENDUM MAY HAVE TO BE ESTABLISHED TO ENABLE A NEW SOCIAL SECURITY FUND TO BE CREATED AND TO ESTABLISH A NATIONAL HYDROGEN INDUSTRY.

At the present, there is no such entity as a Social Security Fund, for the fund was abolished, and the Social Security money was rechanneled to the general fund. Lyndon B. Johnson engineered the "looting of the Social Security Money" to kill more Vietnamese in the ungodly war against the tiny nation of Vietnam. Therefore, new laws must protect the Social Security money paid in by workers from government liars, thieves, and self-styled "Caesars."

FOLLOWING IS MY PLAN

From government records in April 2006, each wage earner pays 12.4 percent of his or her wages into Social Security. That amount is divided in half, so the employer pays 6.2 percent and the wage earner pays 6.2 percent.

My plan is based upon the past, present, and future conditions.

Since the self-styled "Caesars" in Washington took the people's Social Security money for Caesar exploits and began to give the working people's money to people that never paid into the fund, a new perspective must be initiated that will protect Social Security money and be just.

FREEDOM AND WEALTH FOR AMERICANS CAN FLOW AS "MILK AND HONEY."

My fair and good plan for America would divide the amount paid into a new Social Security Fund into three 5-percent parts. The wage earner would have 5 percent of his or her wages withheld to a Social Security Fund. That 5 percent deduction should be matched by 5 percent from the employer and 5 percent should be matched by the FEDERAL GOVERNMENT'S GENERAL FUND

Remember, readers and fellow Americans, the Social Security money was stolen by "self-styled Caesars" to conduct the Vietnam and Korean Wars and by giving the SS money to those that never paid in a dime. The government's new payroll deduction for retirement security was named the Federal Insurance Contributions Act, referred to as FICA. It was written so that the money that goes into FICA can be disbursed to millions of people that never paid a dime into the fund.

ENEMIES OF THE PEOPLE

Using American's money for "Caesar exploits" in grand ploys to interfere into the internal affairs of foreign nations was and is counterproductive to world development.

Killing 500,000 Vietnamese, 50,000 Americans, plus one million Chinese and Koreans in wild Caesar exploits was criminal to the people of the world, especially the Vietnamese, Koreans, Chinese, and the Americans that were duped into being used as pawns.

It is now time to restrict "Caesar exploits," balance the federal budget, retrieve our SS money, and protect the SS Fund from government thieves, eliminate a trade deficit, and create the changes that will enable Americans to get the "fruits of their own labors."

A Balanced Budget Amendment with a proviso that all federal elected representatives would forfeit a year's pay if the yearly budget is not balanced would be a big change to increase the wealth of Americans.

Also, another change is necessary. At the present time, a person pays SS money only to a $90,000-a-year income. That should be changed to be: a person pays SS on their income to ten million dollars a year. All they make over ten million would be free from a SS deduction.

That should be open for change as inflation decreases the value of the dollar.

Therefore, my gift of a capital-generating program that will be the greatest monetary philanthropic gift in the history of humanity will guarantee Americans greater freedom and wealth as never known before.

MORE MONEY COULD FLOW TO THE SOCIAL SECURITY FUND.

I submit a new NATIONAL HYDROGEN INDUSTRY to be created that would be 49-percent owned by a new Social Security Administration. All the present oil companies and pipeline companies that pipe natural gas and petroleum would be given the opportunity to be the 51-percent owners of the NATIONAL HYDROGEN INDUSTRY. After the corporation would be formed, it should be closed so no other company could distribute hydrogen in America.

NON-POLITICAL MANAGERS SHOULD MANAGE THE PROPOSED SOCIAL SECURITY FUND.

I suggest nine administrators manage the SS Fund for terms of six years, three from the major religions in America, three from labor unions, and three from business. The first nine to be appointed by the president, and subsequent administrators to be chosen by the outgoing administrators. The first administrators should have their terms staggered, in two-year periods, so that six always have experience. Their salary should be set to be twelve times the national minimum hourly wage, with no excessive traveling expenses.

BILLIONS OF DOLLARS COULD FLOW TO THE SS FUND.

With billions and billions of dollars flowing into the SS Fund, the administrators should be given the power to determine the amount of money paid to retirees and be able to assume some or all expenses for the elderly now under Medicare.

In addition, patents will enable the National Hydrogen Industry to license electrolyzers to be used by other nations. For nineteen years, profits from the licenses would add additional moneys to the SS Fund. In addition, the administrators should be empowered to make acquisitions of other businesses that are in the energy business. For example, geothermal electrical-generating plants in Western America. Plus the ability to have built electrical-generating plants powered with hydrogen, IF private industry does not keep energy supply with energy demand.

However, the administrators should be denied the power to invest the Social Security money in junk bonds, futures, and any risk derivatives.

This great gift that I propose should not be blocked by any politician or any "buccaneering capitalist."

If my gift to the American people is delayed for any reason, a NATIONAL REFERENDUM may be needed. In that case, a National Hydrogen Industry should be created by the government and 100-percent owned by the Social Security Fund. If this becomes necessary, the National Hydrogen Industry should be NATIONALIZED so that no company could build electrolyzers or distribute hydrogen in competition to the Nationalized Hydrogen Industry. However, at the end of twenty years, an IPO should be offered to companies that would be the distributors of hydrogen.

A fifty-one percent share of the stock should be offered in order to preserve American capitalism. Hopefully, this course of action would not be necessary. However, no business or person should prevent this gift to the American people from being realized.

MANY NOW RECEIVING SS BENEFITS WOULD NOT BE ELIGIBLE.

Millions of Americans, recent immigrants, and others collecting benefits that never paid in a dime would lose SS benefits. However, Congress could and should create a special fund taken from the general fund for welfare people and those under Medicaid.

ADDITIONAL BENEFITS

By using hydrogen to power internal combustion engines and turbines, the chief cause for the "Earth Warming" effect would no longer exist.

The chief cause for "Earth Warming" and smog is from carbon dioxide and the solid particulates vented into the atmosphere via emissions from coal-powered electrical-generating plants and the exhaust from gasoline—and diesel-powered internal combustion engines. Electrical-generating plants that use coal are responsible for about 40 percent of the gases that cause "Earth Warming," chiefly carbon dioxide and, to a lesser degree, methane.

Therefore, in the short term, acid rain would cease as hydrogen replaces low-grade coal—that is, coal with a high content of sulfur. In the long term, fossil fuel industries will be phased out as the new economic structure becomes adjusted to being hydrogen powered. Therefore, coal will eventually be completely replaced as an energy source.

Hydrogen-powered electrical-generating plants can be built for desalination plants where fresh water is scarce as in the LA region and Northern China.

One-thousand-mile and 1,500-mile Maglev trains can be built from Virginia to Harrisburg, Pittsburgh, Erie, Rochester, on the west leg and to Baltimore, Philadelphia, New Jersey, New York, and Boston on the right leg by building electrical-generating plants every hundred miles that can be powered by hydrogen. We could have built this with the money that was spent on George W. Bush's Iraq fiasco.

LARGE-SCALE MILITARY CONFLICTS CAN BE ENDED.

Perhaps the greatest benefit to all humanity by switching to hydrogen can be subdued warfare or general world peace. Slowly, peace could envelope the world, for the Muslim terrorist nations would slowly have a decline in dollars and be forced to create new businesses. Muslims would be free to live as the Koran dictates without the interference of American self-styled "Caesars."

Therefore, consideration number one: with hydrogen to power internal combustion engines and electrical-generating plants, any Muslim nation's program to enrich uranium would be unnecessary UNLESS the uranium is to be used to make atomic bombs. Consideration number two: why would an oil-rich nation such as Iran want fission material when they have plenty of oil to power electrical-generation plants UNLESS they want to make atomic bombs? Consideration number three: why would Muslim nations want to make and own atomic bombs? Answer: to use them or sell them to a terrorist group so they can use them.

I state truly and emphatically, no Muslim or rogue nation should be permitted to possess atomic bombs. However, looking to the future, if Pakistan is taken over by a fundamentalist coup, they would inherit the atomic bombs. This would necessitate a severe response.

It is out of the scope of this work to speculate about the responses to a rogue nation with atomic bombs.

However, in regard to peace in the world, there will always be conflicts between tribes and groups. At the beginning of the twenty-first century, there are people (Muslims) that have plural wives and deny women equal rights. Sunnis and Shiites kill each other in sectarian violence. In Madagascar, the non-Christians exhume the dead every five to seven years to dance with the corpse. In Borneo, there are headhunters and cannibals. Nelson Rockefeller's son was either beheaded or eaten by a primitive tribe. Also, sad but true, different Christian denominations are so intolerant to each other that murders are committed during religious conflicts. Therefore, as Christians believe, only when Christ returns will there be complete world peace, and as Jewish people believe, only when the Messiah comes will there be complete world peace.

This concludes chapter one. Remember, only by political pressure from the general public will this great gift to the American people be realized. Chapter two is devoted to WHY America bears the brunt of terrorist attacks, including WHY the Twin Towers were destroyed.

CHAPTER TWO

IT IS IMPORTANT TO REVIEW AMERICAN HISTORY TO DETERMINE THE CAUSES FOR THE TWIN TOWERS' DESTRUCTION. DESTINY UNFOLDS AS EVERY ACTION CREATES A REACTION.

Since the beginning of time, when physical matter was created and began motion, action created a reaction.

This fact became a law of science when Isaac Newton (1642-1727) gave to the world his three laws of motion. The third law states: "To every action, there is an equal and opposite reaction." However, within the affairs of individuals, groups, and nations, an action and reaction law exists and is very sensitive to the finest increment. It is known as THE LAW OF RECOMPENSE.

The Law of Recompense, known also from the verse "as ye sow, so shall ye reap," and from Moses the lawgiver from about 1300 BC, where he warned about reactions from committing offences against another person. Exodus KJV 24. "Eye for eye, tooth for tooth, hand for hand, foot for foot,

25. Burning for burning, wound for wound, stripe for stripe.

Leviticus

19. And if a man cause a blemish in his neighbour; as he hath done, so shall it be done to him;
20. Breach for breach, eye for eye, tooth for tooth: as he hath caused a blemish in a man, so shall it be done to him again."

"An eye for an eye—a tooth for a tooth" is a valid psychological or spiritual law that exacts retribution for offenses and exacts rewards for constructive deeds. As ye sow, so shall ye reap—a person or nation that sows sparingly, reaps sparingly, AND conversely, those that sow plentifully, reap plentifully. The effect from actions or reaping operates in the energies of the unconscious mind, the Akasha (a-ka-sha) of all men and women and collectively through a nation.

PROJECTION AND ATTRACTION

There is a continual projection of ideas and actions into the collective unconscious mind of all humanity, the Stegokar or Akasha energy. This causes a psychological or spiritual attraction to balance the projection force. Thus, as ye sow, so shall ye reap, to the finest increment—that is, to every jot and tittle.

NOTHING JUST HAPPENS; EVERYTHING IS CAUSED.

In the science of psychology, this action reaction is called determinism. From a spiritual perspective, this action-reaction, projection-attraction is called the Law of Recompense.

All the activities of nature and man are stored in the skein of time and space (Stegokar—explained in volumes two and three of my major work) and have been read by a few down through the centuries. The records have been called the BOOK OF REMEMBRANCE. (Malachi 3:16, KJV) "Then they that feared the LORD spake often one to another: and the LORD hearkened, and heard it, and a book of remembrance was written before him for them that feared the LORD, and that thought upon his name."

The Hindu religion refers to the "Book of Remembrance" as the Akashic records.

THE TWIN TOWERS DESTROYED, OVER THREE THOUSAND PEOPLE KILLED.

In America, about two thirds of the populace believe in God, and many have wondered how and why God could have allowed such destruction. The truth is evident. God created physical and spiritual laws to assist earthbound souls in attaining oneness in consciousness with our creator. God does not violate these laws. Christ has the keys to God's laws, and only through Christ can exceptions be made.

TOO MANY PEOPLE IN AMERICA HAVE LOST THE ONENESS THEY HAD WITH GOD AND HAVE PUT THEIR TRUST IN THE FEDERAL GOVERNMENT.

It is the operation of the Law of Recompense that enabled the motive for the terrorist attacks on the Twin Towers on September 11, 2001, in New York.

A great attractive force was set in America's Akasha or its Stegokar psyche or the nation's collective unconscious mind. That is why America was attacked on September 11, 2001. The cause or the sowing or great offences set in the Akasha can be chiefly traced to the atrocities committed against the Vietnamese people and to the Chinese and Korean people in the American crimes against humanity during the wars with Vietnam and Korea.

However, there has been a continual build up of ungodly actions in the Akasha, beginning with the war against England in 1812, the war against Spain, declaring war on the Austro-Hungarian Empire on December 7, 1917, the war against Vietnam, Korea, Somalia, and now Iraq.

As ye sow, so shall ye reap has been stated in modern lingo as *that which goes around, comes around.*

The mortal mind is unable to accurately connect very great misfortunes to causes. However, some changes that carry destructive consequences can be connected. If the politicians in Washington had declared war on Spain in a land-grabbing ploy, America would not have had an influx of semideveloped people from the Caribbean. The effects of declaring war on the Austro-Hungarian Empire on December 7, 1917, came back on exactly the same month and day—December 7, 1941.

More recently, the Waco massacre that occurred on April 19, 1994, was directly responsible for two following terrorist attacks. Timothy McVeigh was at the Waco compound when the tank rammed the building and set fire to the building. Timothy McVeigh was traumatized at that sight, and it allowed an evil, schizophrenic alter ego to form, i.e., an ID schizoid. It is no doubt that Bill Clinton and Janet Reno were responsible for the Waco massacre and became an integral part of the schizoid that formed in Timothy McVeigh's mind. The excess destruction and cruelty at Waco disturbed the Akasha, and as a meteor striking the ocean, a tidal wave is a natural consequence.

Therefore, if there had not been a Waco massacre, the Alfred P. Murrah building in Oklahoma would not have been bombed. Also, on October 9, 1995, the sabotaging of the train the Sunset Limited near Hyder, Arizona, would not have occurred.

The root causes for the Murrah building bombing and the Sunset Limited train derailment are in the actions of Bill Clinton and Janet Reno.

Warren Jeffs, the polygamist, had numerous compounds in Colorado and Arizona; it was reported that he had 10,000 followers. He was wanted by the FBI and was captured in Las Vegas on August 29, 2006.

Some of his wives escaped, and one gave a gruesome tale of life in a polygamist's compound. However, no massacre occurred, for none of his compounds were destroyed by federal tanks and firebombs. Therefore, no great recompense will come to America.

THE URGE FOR RICHES AND FREEDOM IS UNIVERSAL.
COLONIALISM WAS A METHOD TO MAKE PROFIT FROM

UNDERDEVELOPED NATIONS. IN THE PROCESS, IT SPREAD
CIVILIZATION. HOWEVER, THE DESIRE TO BE FREE FROM A
COLONIAL POWER EMERGED AS EACH NATION DEVELOPED.

After WW II, the Vietnam people wanted freedom from France since Vietnam
was part of the colonial possessions in Southeast Asia. President Truman was asked
by Vietnam leaders to assist Vietnam to become a free nation. President Truman
and probably his advisors informed the Vietnam dignitaries that France owned
Vietnam, and the United States agreed with France. The leader of Vietnam, Ho
Chi Minh, made at least one personal visit to Washington, DC, to see President
Truman to gain his support to end the French imperialism or colonialism in
Vietnam. Ho Chi Minh wanted national freedom or Vietnamese independence
from the French. Unfortunately for all humanity, President Truman would not
see Ho Chi Minh. So the leader of this tiny Southeast Asian nation went home
very disappointed, but it is recorded, and motion pictures of the event do exist
that "Ho," as he became known, read a paraphrased American Declaration of
Independence in the central square of Hanoi.

Ho Chi Minh begged on bended knee to Archemedes who was, at that time,
Harry Truman's emissary to Vietnam for assistance to become a free nation. Ah!
Washington did communicate to "Ho" and told him that Vietnam was a French
possession.

"Ho" had a fondness for Americans and continued a fervent plea through
government channels for support to gain Vietnamese independence. Washington
warned "Ho" that Vietnam belonged to France, and American troops would be
increased in Vietnam if they got hostile in their efforts to become independent.
"Ho" was very, very disappointed and returned the warning by stating that Russia
would help Vietnam gain independence if Washington did not support their
efforts to become an independent nation.

Cocky, pugilistic President Truman responded by increasing American
military troops in Vietnam to enforce French rule, and thus President Truman
started the Vietnam War.

In 1954, the Vietnamese defeated the French at Dien Bien Phu, and the
self-styled "Caesars" in Washington increased the illegal war against Vietnam. It
was constitutionally illegal because Congress never declared war on Vietnam.

"IN GOD WE TRUST" WAS PUT ASIDE IN FAVOR OF KILLING,
TORTURE, AND BURNING ALIVE LITTLE CHILDREN WITH
NAPALM.

After fifty years, the brutalities committed against the Filipino people by
American armed forces was to be repeated in another Asian nation, Vietnam,

for the same reason—to deny them independence—but this time with greater brutality.

After American troop strength was increased in Vietnam, the Vietnamese people were stimulated by an increased desire for freedom and independence, and it was only a matter of months for Vietnam to prepare a military strength that would be strong enough to begin guerilla warfare against the intruding American military forces. God favored the Vietnamese people, and the American "Caesars" became "conquest crazed."

From the period following WW II, American military forces occupied Vietnam for the sole purpose of keeping Vietnam a colonial possession of France. Later, it became an obsession to defeat a military force that made war on American forces.

Slowly, the resolve to be free strengthened the Vietnamese people for over a decade.

Self-styled "Caesars" in Washington continued to increase brutalities against Vietnam. Finally, on April 30, 1975, the last Americans departed from Saigon, and the war was over.

The Vietnamese people suffered horribly. The American forces killed 500,000 Vietnamese and dropped one ton of Agent Orange for every 100 Vietnamese. After the war, 500,000 Vietnamese babies were born with birth defects from the effects of Agent Orange. America has done nothing in the form of reparations to pay for the destruction wrought upon their nation.

THE DESTRUCTION AND MASSACRES UPON THAT SMALL NATION WAS GROSSLY UNGODLY.

A great imbalance was created by the projection of thoughts and deeds into the energies that hold the memories in the unconscious mind of all humanity, or the Akasha, that must be balanced. Tooth for tooth, eye for eye, the degree of destruction projected against the Vietnam nation would cause an attraction of destruction to the offender, America, to the finest increment or to every "jot and tittle."

GOOD THOUGHTS AND DEEDS ATTRACTS IN RETURN GOOD THOUGHTS AND DEEDS. EVIL THOUGHTS AND DEEDS ATTRACT IN RETURN EVIL THOUGHTS AND DEEDS.

Only evil can come from anything founded on evil. Only ill fortune was generated upon the psyche of the American nation from the atrocities to the Vietnamese people. Because of that principle, not only was President Truman's idea to start the Vietnam war based upon a demonic premise, from that military involvement, a powerful negative psychological force was generated that increased the existing schizophrenic "war-crazed" mental state of American politicians, AND it would spread and grow in the minds of the American psyche. My in-depth characterization of President Truman is a "cocky, pugilistic piker."

PRESIDENT TRUMAN THEN INTERFERED INTO THE INTERNAL AFFAIRS OF KOREA BY ENGAGING AMERICA IN A MILITARY ACTION THAT HE SAID WAS MERELY A "POLICE ACTION."

Korea was having very similar development problems just as America had that led to the Civil War. In Korea, the North favored a communist government while the South favored a democratic government. In America, the South favored an economy powered by slaves. The North favored an economy powered by free citizens.

As we review our nation's development, slavery was grossly evil, and the two economic systems could not continue. Young America was having great development problems. It was morally right and good for America to solve our development problems ourselves without any outside interference.

Vietnam and Korea should have been allowed to solve their own development problems. However, from the growing "Caesar" mentality in Washington, evil politicians craved to "Rule the World" from Washington.

All the pain, misery, and abuses perpetrated upon the peoples of Cuba, the Philippines, Vietnam, Korea, China, Somalia, and Iraq are registered in the unconscious mind of humanity, the Akasha, AND they must be balanced by the Law of Recompense.

INTERFERING INTO THE INTERNAL AFFAIRS OF FOREIGN NATIONS WAS AND IS REGISTERED.

Only by going to God and Christ and asking for forgiveness for these ungodly acts can the recompense be shunted to the self-styled "Caesar" politicians that are responsible for the crimes against humanity.

Ask yourself the following questions: Did the terrible destruction to Vietnam bring forth any good? Is Korea better and more stable since the American intervention? Is Somalia better since the American interference? Is Iraq better since American destruction and the freeing of hostile groups to wage war upon each other as they did for centuries?

From the great damage heaped upon Iraq, the nation is fractured and is ripe for another coup where another strongman can gain control, as did Saddam Hussein.

Turkey's leader or the Justice and Development Party said, "Iraq elections won't be democratic and are unlikely to stem violence."

If Iraq would be divided into three sections—Sunni, Shiite, and Kurd—it *may* be the least painful for developing Iraq. However, a large section of the western desert should be ceded to Arabia to keep Israel a safe distance from Scud missiles.

SCHOOLS IN IRAQ

Iraqi children are being educated by teaching them the Koran. In a generation, Iraq will become a Muslim fundamentalist country.

CAESAR RULE IS CRIMINAL TO THE WORLD'S PEOPLE.

The idea to rule the world from Washington is criminal. Each nation should be allowed to develop at their own pace.

The self-styled "Caesars" in Washington claim the Iraq war is all about fighting terrorism. That is a blatant LIE. The reason for the war has changed from "Saddam has weapons of mass destruction" to fighting terrorism. Fortunately for America, most Americans know that George W. Bush is a LIAR.

As with Vietnam before, many of the Iraqi people see the American forces as interlopers and won't be satisfied until all foreign military forces get out of Iraq.

However, the Washington self-styled "Caesars" have used lies to justify the invasion of Iraq. Therefore, the question should be answered: are the American and foreign forces liberators or interlopers?

THIS QUESTION SHOULD BE SETTLED IN A DEMOCRATIC MANNER

It is claimed that democracy is to be established in Iraq. If that were true, the following national vote of the Iraqi people would settle that question. Do you want the American and foreign forces TO STAY or GET OUT?

However, as honest and democratic as a national vote can be, it would be a 180-degree-turn for the self-styled "Caesars" in Washington if they honored the will of the Iraqi people. It is more likely that they would not allow the Iraqi people to decide that issue by a referendum, because Washington's self-styled "Caesars" want to rule the world from Washington.

Devil Driven is my assessment of the self-styled "Caesars" that heaped upon the American people the effects from the wars that is mentioned in this work. War on Spain, the Austro-Hungarian Empire, Vietnam, Korea, Somalia, and the Iraq war. Only the war to chase the Iraqi forces out of Kuwait was just (not considering WWII, where we were attacked, and Hitler declared war on America.)

WARS AND RUMORS OF WAR.

Conflicts in families, tribes, and nations are old as humanity. The reasons for conflicts have not changed. These are: a craving to rule others, a desire to steal wealth from another nation, a clash of cultures (religion is a facet of culture), and an inferiority complex.

If emotionally instability is added to any of these conditions—the idea of using force against others to achieve greater-than-thee status (superiority)—violence emerges as a way to settle differences.

However, "to every action there is an equal and opposite reaction." Thus, a chain of events is created that are bound together by the law "as ye sow, so shall ye reap."

DESTINY UNFOLDS BY DRIVING MENTAL FORCES

To understand more clearly how the Law of Recompense operates through and by the Akasha or the total unconscious mind or all humanity, it is important to realize that although the individual minds of all humanity are one part of the total collective unconscious mind, the Akasha is stratified. Therefore, to make the explanation easy to understand, the Akasha has two major divisions. These are the forces of good and the forces of evil. These forces, though stratified in the Akasha, do interact with each other to prevent the forces of evil from dominating. All the spiritual laws of God the Father or our creator have been formulated to assist all souls to return in consciousness to their creator.

For example, Timothy McVeigh may have been a borderline godly person before he watched the Waco massacre. However, after seeing the tank attack the compound and the firebombs lobbed into the building, his hatred for the federal government led to a dominating idea to punish the government for the massacre. When this occurred in his mind, he created a split or schizophrenic condition in his mind.

ID SCHIZOPHRENIA

In classic schizophrenia, an alter ego can and does assume dominance by taking over the "seat of consciousness." However, that schizophrenic condition develops in phases, whereas when a person becomes obsessed with an abnormal idea, the obsession can become so intense that a possession occurs without an alter ego taking over the "seat of consciousness."

All the basal emotions in a person are animalistic and are encapsulated in a kernel somewhere in the medulla. The kernel and the energies that sustain the kernel is the ID.

As humanity becomes more refined, the selfish and cruel ID nature from an ancient past loses its power to influence the mind. However, the ID is present in the mind and can be aroused when self-discipline does not contain the wild, selfish, and cruel cravings.

When wild, selfish, and cruel cravings are intentionally created, an alter ego is created that has its roots in the ID. When this occurs, the alter ego is ID created, and it uses the same ego in the "seat of consciousness" as the normal awake mind. Therefore, to give two examples, Ted Bundy and Timothy McVeigh had ID schizophrenia.

I realize the explanation of ID schizophrenia is new.

However, in the third volume of my major work, this topic is considered carefully.

Moses spoke of ID schizophrenia, for it is recorded in Deuteronomy 28:43, "The stranger that is within thee shall get up above thee very high; and thou shalt come down very low. 44: He shall lend to thee, and thou shalt not lend to him: he shall be the head, and thou shalt be the tail."

STRANGER WITHIN THEE, AN EVIL ID SCHIZOID

Since Timothy McVeigh was at the Waco massacre on April 19, 1994, and intentionally created a burning hatred with a revenge intent, his mind shunted these thoughts to a new circuitry, and his obsession created an ID schizophrenic secondary of double self, i.e, an ID SCHIZOID.

As this was occurring, the vibration rate of the second self was registered in the Akasha or the collective unconscious mind of humanity. This caused his place in the stratified Akasha to be changed to agree with the new vibration rate. In short, his mind became unified with the lowest, or evil, strata.

THE LAW OF RECOMPENSE—AS YE SOW, SO SHALL YE REAP—IS A LAW AS ALL THE LAWS OF THE UNIVERSE, AS GRAVITY, FOR EXAMPLE.

God does not punish humanity; we punish ourselves. The Law of Recompense operates as a psychological force, just as physical forces operate that cause earthquakes, volcanoes, hurricanes, and tornadoes. Every earthly event and, from a larger view, galactic event is caused.

Among all the teachings in the New Testament, it teaches to be moderate. In this manner, excesses do not cause retribution.

ISLAM STUDIED

Since this chapter is focused on the destruction of the Twin Towers and terrorist attacks against civilized nations, an analysis of Islam and Muslim people will reveal the character of those dedicated to destructive acts against Christians, Jews, and Hindus.

CHAPTER THREE

WHO ARE THE ARABS? WHAT IS THEIR NATURE?

Since the destruction of the Twin Towers on September 11, 2001, great interest has been generated to look into the psyche of the people that perpetrated the destructive acts and of those that danced in the streets at America's great pain.

Who are the Arabs is a question on the mind of many Americans. This question about the Arabs pertains to their genetic lineage. The Internet abounds with texts that focus on the Arabs. Who are the Arabs and the origin of jihad are two questions that sources on Google abundantly respond to.

The ancient roots of Jewish and Arab people began with a very wealthy herdsman in the Mediterranean region, probably Iraq. His name was Abram, whose name was changed by God to Abraham. His people were of a tribe known as Semites and moved often to find the best grazing land for their herds. According to biblical text, Abraham's wife, Sarah, had a slave, called a handmaiden or maid, named Hagar. Abraham fathered a son by Hagar named Ishmael. He was Abraham's oldest son. However, this son and his progeny were to be a problem for all humanity.

God revealed to Moses that an angel of the Lord had spoken to Hagar and revealed the nature of the child she would bear that was still in her womb. An account of this is given in Genesis, chapter 16, verses eleven and twelve. Eleventh verse: "And the angel of the LORD said unto her, Behold, thou art with child, and shalt bear a son, and shalt call his name Ishmael; because the LORD hath heard thy affliction." Twelfth verse: "And he will be a wild man; his hand will be against every man, and every man's hand against him; and he shall dwell in the presence of all his brethren."

Moses spoke to God, and through this communication, God gave Moses many truths, including the Ten Commandments. In addition, God revealed to Moses that Ishmael was predisposed to be a nature person or, as God revealed to Moses, a "wild man."

ABRAHAM SIRES ANOTHER SON.

Then, Abraham fathered a son by Sarah, his wife, named Isaac. This son sired two sons, named Jacob and Essau.

The tribes of Israel were formed after Abraham's grandson; Jacob (son of Isaac) had his name changed by God to Israel. Jacob had six sons by one wife and two sons each by three concubines. These twelve sons became the leader of their own families, and as the families grew, they eventually became the twelve tribes of Israel. The son by Abraham's wife's servant, Ishmael, became the leader of his clan, named the Ishmaelites.

Pure Arabs can trace their lineage to Abraham and Hagar. Thus, about four thousand years ago, from the seed of Abraham, two distinct and different tribes began. These were the tribes of the Israelites and the tribes of the Ishmaelites.

In order to address the nature of the Arabs, it will be quite helpful if the reference to Ishmael being a "wild Man" is not considered. Therefore, by comparing Ishmaelites to other tribes, their innate nature can be revealed.

Also useful in analyzing innate natures is the use of the well-known quote from the New Testament, "By their fruits, ye shall know them."

Therefore, the vital information in determining the innate nature of a person, tribe, or a nation is determined by examining their emotional stability and intellectual accomplishments.

ABRAHAM DIED, AND THE CENTURIES PASSED.

After the death of Abraham, the Israelites and the Ishmaelites brought forth many children and wandered independently as herdsmen. About eight hundred years after Abraham died, the Israeli people experienced the first of three momentous events that changed their destiny forever. The first event that caused great changes to the Israeli people was the birth and leadership of Moses. The second event was the forty years of rigorous survival methods experienced in the Sinai Desert while trusting Moses and praying to God for help in order to survive the harsh environment.

These struggles caused the proteins that are created by genes to form new configurations to be ingrained or set firmly that could be passed to their offspring. At the end of the forty-year struggle, every Israeli that departed Egypt was dead, and two new generations would leave the desert with a new leader, Joshua.

Meanwhile, the Ishmaelites were tending their flocks as they wandered in search of better lands for their herds.

The two events experienced by the Israeli tribe had a profound effect that caused greater differences between the Israelites and the Ishmaelites that endure and will endure till the end time of man.

Moses and no doubt his closest associates had a penchant for studying and understanding the human mind. This led to communicating with the highest mind, or God. Thus, God chose them to be his people. However, it was a two-way street, to use a modern term, for they first chose to understand God. The books of

Moses are testimony to the relationship between God and man upon the earth. The fact that the books of Moses were written on animal skins several hundred years after the death of Moses is another testimony that his followers were able communicators with God the father.

This is important in understanding the nature of the Israeli and Ishmaelite people.

While the Israelites were experiencing formative events to their tribal consciousness, the Ishmaelites were without any similar mind-altering forces.

The result of the differences produced two tribes as different as the American Indian and the Northern European colonists.

SELF-DISCIPLINE IS A STRONG TRAIT OF ISRAELITES

The Israelites became creative intellectuals, with a trait to exercise "self-discipline" in order to obey the laws given by Moses. In addition, from their struggles in the Sinai Desert, a trait was formed to hold to all they gained.

In 1312 BC, Israel became a nation. King David founded the new nation and made Jerusalem the capital. That was almost two thousand years before Mohammed, the founder of Islam, was born.

SELF-DISCIPLINE IS NOTABLY MISSING IN ISHMAELITES

The Ishmaelites can best be described as nature people. They were more emotional in behavior, without the controlled use of self-discipline. This innate nature is the reason God told Hagar her unborn son, to be named Ishmael, would have a wild nature.

These different emotional natures between the Israelites and the Ishmaelites are still evident today, for the Ishmaelites will riot and bring destruction to lands where they dwell and to their own national utilities while the Israelites will *not* riot and strive to maintain social order.

FROM THE BEGINNING

The Israelites sought to change the conditions of the environment for their survival. Stone and brick buildings were built with great expertise.

Remnants of their early work still stand, whereas the Ishmaelites lived in tents and identified with the environment, as is the custom with nature people. They lived a nomadic life, always moving to find something better that nature could provide for them.

Ishmael's progeny also divided into tribes, and after centuries of wanderings through the Middle East by the tribes of Ishmael, the Greek writer Herodotus in the sixth century BC wrote of a people that inhabited the Arabian Peninsula. He observed that these people were nomads and referred to them as Arabs.

The word, *Arab*, is derived from the Semitic root word relating to nomadism. Thus, the land of Arabia was named after a tribe of Semitic Ishmaelite wanderers or nomads.

Therefore, from then on, the scribes of ancient Greece used the name for Ishmael's descendents as Arabs, and scribes of other tribes copied the name *Arab*, and the name *Ishmaelites* was discontinued.

About six hundred years after the Greek writer Herodotus coined the word Arab for the Ishmaelites, Christ was born in Bethlehem in Judea.

The third great event that altered the lives of Israelites was the rejection of the Messiah. This aspect is considered in my third volume of my major work.

Understanding Judaic laws was easy for the early Israeli intellectuals since they had a penchant for grasping mind science. The Northern Europeans and those with Northern European genes had a mental trait that also enabled them to perceive how the consciousness of man could be altered by God. After Constantine, many European tribes adopted Christianity, and Christianity spread throughout many lands.

TIME PASSES

Centuries passed in the period AD, and the nature of the Ishmaelite-Arabs created a reclusive trait. Polygamy was practiced, and the role of women in their life was devoted to sexually satisfying men. It is a practice that endures to the twenty-first century and causes the chief contention between Muslims and non-Muslims.

Whenever Americans interact with Muslims, the American agitation for political reform that gives women more rights causes fanatical resistance. Muslims will fight and die before they lose the right to have several wives and raise women's rights to be equal to men.

Returning to the Ishmaelite-Arabs, the 1 percent of the intelligentsia ruled the people, and from this small select group, a male child was born in Mecca, Arabia, in the year 571, that was named Elijah Muhammad. The name Muhammad means "the praised one."

Muhammad was born into a society that practiced polygamy. The wealth of an Arab would determine how many wives he could support.

Muhammad's early life was marked by misfortunes. His father died before he was born. According to the findings in my research, Mohammad's mother was a Christian Jewess. Therefore, assuming that other researchers were accurate, Mohammad was a half Jew. Although, according to Jewish genealogy, a child born of a Jewish mother is a Jew.

Muhammad's mother's influence to the young Ishmaelite-Israelite was short-lived, for she died when he was six years old. He than went to live another short-lived life with a grandfather. He died, and when Muhammad was eight, he then went to live with an uncle.

MUHAMMAD GREW INTO MANHOOD.

Muhammad first wife was his employer, a rich widow by the name of Khadija. Islamic records claim that Muhammad married her in 595. She was about fifteen years his senior. They were married for twenty-four years, until her death. Muhammad then married several women that were daughters of tribal leaders. This connection to power figures bestowed importance to himself among other Arabs. According to the records, he married eleven times, once to a six-year-old girl by the name of Ayesha.

It is no doubt that Muhammad had a brilliant mind and had gained great respect, although he never learned to read or write.

When Muhammad was about forty years old, about 610 or 611, it is recorded in Islamic records that he had a visit from Gabriel, the Moon God or reigning spirit of the Moon.

He relayed this story to his first wife, Khadija. She believed Muhammad with absolute faith, and Khadija became Muhammad's first ardent supporter.

According to Islamic records, Gabriel taught Muhammad and claimed that the true religion was lost, and Muhammad was to serve Gabriel and restore the true religion.

In the present world, there are serious questions to this claim. Another possibility has been considered that Muhammad could go into a light trance state where he hallucinated and when coming into normal consciousness could remember what he saw and heard while in the altered state of consciousness.

MUHAMMED GAINED SUPPORTERS.

About 610 or 611, Muhammad became outspoken about a new Islam Brotherhood. Islam means "submission to the will of God." His path to establish this new order was marked by many contentious events. Slowly, he gained followers. When he fell into the altered state, a scribe would write all that Muhammad said that was supposed to have come from Gabriel. The text was copied onto leaves and other material that Muhammad's scribe had used to store the words of Muhammad. The original writings were without order or system. However, the texts were rearranged and stored in scrolls called the Qu'ran, translated to English as Koran.

In 632, Muhammad died, and his stature as a prophet grew rapidly.

For all seekers of truth, I entreat all to go to Google and read the history of Muhammad. You will read of a near-primitive people that invented nothing and would be living a primitive lifestyle, IF they did not use all the electrical devices invented by Christian and Jews.

Muslims firmly believe that Muhammad was a great and good man, and his directives in the Koran are to be obeyed.

The Google site contains a very condensed story of the birth or Muhammad, the rise of Islam, and the death of Muhammad.

THE FOLLOWERS OF ISLAM BELIEVE ISLAM TO BE A RELIGION.

Islam is based upon the Koran. It is a history book with directives that are considered to be spiritual and are to be obeyed. Its followers, therefore, are so vastly different to the followers in other spiritual organizations that it bears no comparison.

Whether Islam is compared to Hinduism, Judaism, Christianity, or Buddhism, Islam stands alone. Excepting Islam, the major religions teach their adherents to be moderate in behavior. In addition, these religions have laws and regimens designed to raise consciousness. In Hinduism, the adherents are taught how to reach a high state of consciousness called Kundalina consciousness and Samadhi. Immortality is a main tenet of Hinduism. Be good to your fellow man, be kind to animals, and the highest afterlife can be achieved.

Judaism and Christianity have laws and regimens designed to raise consciousness. Both of these religions have an unshakable faith in the Holy Ghost or Holy Spirit. From the beginning to the end of both religions, it is taught that the power of the Holy Ghost or Spirit can enhance consciousness and bestow exceptional abilities. In Exodus 31: 3-5, it is written

3. "and I have filled him (Bezale-el) with the spirit of God, in wisdom, and in understanding, and in knowledge, and in all manner of workmanship.
4. To devise cunning works, to work in gold, and in silver, and in brass,
5. And in cutting stones, to set them, and in carving of timber, to work in all manner of workmanship."

Programming of and by the Holy Spirit can bestow exceptional abilities.

In Christianity, Christ taught: (Mat 6:33, KJV) "But seek ye first the kingdom of God, and his righteousness; and all these things shall be added unto you. The kingdom of God is within."

Although Christianity teaches that the kingdom of God is within, in order to enter into the kingdom of God while on this Earth or when leaving the body and going to the kingdom of God somewhere in the heavens, consciousness must be changed or a person must be born again.

Therefore, it is stated unequivocally that the high state of consciousness and power is within the composite mind of everyone.

"It is not I that doeth the work, it is father within me, he doeth the work," said the Lord.

Then another verse: "You would have nothing if it wasn't given unto you by the father."

So Hinduism, Judaism, and Christianity agree from the perspective that being good and doing no harm to your fellow man pleases God, and great are the rewards on Earth and in heaven for those that please God.

Buddhism teaches that a high state of consciousness called Nirvana is bestowed upon those that earned it according to their behavior.

Each religion is believed by its adherents to be the true religion above or before other religions. However, Hinduism, Judaism, Christianity, and Buddhism are tolerant to other religions. Islam is not only intolerant to other religions, Muslims are ordered to KILL all those that are not Muslims.

The Muslim ideology or Islam has no development path for its adherents to reach higher consciousness. However, if a devotee becomes a martyr while using his body as a kamikaze bomb and kills many Christians, Jews, Hindus, or Buddhists, he firmly and mistakenly believes that the creator named Allah to Muslims will reward him or her for the murders.

KORAN QUOTES

The following is a quote from the Koran chapter nine and verse twenty-nine. It is made very clear for Muslims to use violence and commit murder.

"Fight these people of the book who do not believe in God and the last day," (that is, their concept of their God) "who do not prohibit what God and his apostle" (Mohammed) "have forbidden, nor accept divine law, until all of them pay protective tax in submission."

Protective tax (jaziyah) means a tax is to levied on non-Muslims for protection and other services. Thus, just as a Mafia protective racket in old New York, all non-Muslims that are not killed are to be subdued and made to pay tax to the Muslim organization.

In addition to the decree to fight all non-Muslims until all non-Muslims submit to Islam and pay to them a tax, consider what is given in the Qur'an or Koran section 12 starts with 88.

"They but wish that ye should reject Faith, as they do, and this be on the same footing (as they); but take not friends from their ranks until they flee in the way of Allah (from what is forbidden.) But if they turn renegades, seize them and slay them; and (in any case) take no friends or helpers from their ranks;"

Muslims are not to take non-Muslims as friends unless they accept Islam. If some do accept Islam and change their mind afterward, they are to be hunted and killed wherever they are found. That sounds difficult to believe at the beginning of the twenty-first century, but the truth concerning this matter follows. If a Muslim converts to another faith, that person is regarded as an "apostate." If a Muslim judge—that is, a Muslim cleric—finds the person guilty of defecting, and others uphold the clerical ruling in a formal ruling, any Muslim is authorized to kill the Muslim defector.

If a Muslim girl dates a man not chosen by the family, she is in danger of being killed, and sometimes by her own brothers. Many young Muslim girls are killed every year for this reason.

If these uncivilized acts seem to be from the Cro-Magnon days, consider the following primitive or criminal Muslim idea that exists in a civilized world. Muslim clerics have a unique power that is not found in any other religious or philosophic organization. Any Muslim cleric or imam is empowered by the Islamic laws to issue a legal ruling to all Muslims (called a FATWA) to war against all non-Muslims in what is called a jihad, or holy war.

Muslims have felt a threat and intimidation to their culture for several decades before the turn of the twenty-first century. In response to this, a holy war against Christians and Jews has been slowly growing. After the New York Twin Towers were leveled by terrorist attacks, the American government promised retaliation, and the search for Osama bin Laden began in Afghanistan. In the third week of October after the search for Osama bin Laden began, an Afghan mulla, imam, or cleric stated, "We are not afraid of death, because martyrdom is a gift of God, and every Muslim aspires to gain the status of martyr." It is the same dedication to dying as the kamikaze pilots did for the Japanese warlords.

Of course, the mullas, Osama bin Laden, and his close associates try to escape the American military. Becoming a martyr is not for the leaders but for those that can be used as pawns.

PRIMITIVE BEHAVIOR

In Africa, some Muslims have a practice of cutting out the clitoris of young girls. In the year 1977, in Arabia, an Arabian princess was killed in Center Square for the crime of infidelity.

However, not all Muslims are hardhearted and are willing to kill and commit terrorist attacks on Christians and Jews. There are some very law-abiding Muslims and some that are timid.

When a poll was taken in England after the bus and subway bombings, over 40 percent of the Muslims polled approved of committing terrorist attacks on

Christian and Jews. On the front page of the *Wall Street Journal* on Thursday, September 28, 2006, the results of a poll taken by University of Maryland revealed a more startling statistic. An Iraqi poll found 60 percent of those polled favor attacking Americans.

MUSLIMS OBEY THE KORAN

A true Muslim will obey the Koran, and the Koran states plainly kill infidels—that is, kill Christians, Jews, and Hindus.

I repeat a comparison of Muslims to the early American Indians. Muslims will eagerly use all the products produced by Christian nations to kill the very people that invented and produced them.

Muslims have not built steel mills, modern chemical plants, and have not invented any electronic devices. However, they will use electricity and all the electronic devices powered by electricity to sustain and advance their culture and their religion. Only a very small percentage of Muslims will make any great change in their culture. They will die before they give up plural marriages and give their women rights compared to men.

However, a greater threat is laid upon Muslims that is firmly believed. The Koran states more than a hundred times to Muslims if any Muslim rejects Mohammad's messages, they will go to HELL. The Koran states: take not the Jews and Christians as friends, Christian and Jews will go to HELL.

The fantasy believed by Muslims that Islam is the one and only true religion and the entire world is to be converted to an Islamic world is ludicrous.

Only by obliterating all Christians, Jews, and Hindus could this fantasy be achieved.

Suppose it happened, who would operate all the technological machines that power the electronic infrastructure? Who would build and operate steel mills, airplanes, automobiles, farm equipment, and communication systems? How much advancement would there be in overcoming diseases?

MUSLIM INVENTIONS

On the net, through Google, one Muslim blogger tries to convince any and all that Muslims are great inventors. He states that Muslims invented glass, the telescope, and mathematics. The truth about glass is abundant, for not only did the Romans have glassblown novelties, the glassblowers of Alexandria Egypt were excellent glass artisans over a thousand years before Mohammad was born. A Dutch Jew spectacle maker, Hans Lippershey, had built a telescope in 1608. In that same year, in Holland, he applied for a patent for a telescope. One year later, Galileo built his first telescope. It was Galileo that made the telescope famous.

A FALSE IDEA STILL CIRCULATES THAT ISHMAELITES OR ARABS INVENTED MATHEMATICS.

Ancient Egyptians, Babylonians, Greeks, and the Indus people—that is, the Sanskrit people—were mathematicians. The people of the Indus Valley along the Indus River were living in that region four hundred thousand years ago. The civilization that developed and used the Sanskrit language and our universal number system started about 2,500 BC. Therefore, our number system was developed five to seven hundred years before Abraham was born. For all people that mistakenly believe that the Arabs created our number system, the following paragraphs pertinent to the history of our number system reveals the origin of mathematics.

The ancient people that dwelled along the Indus River and in the Indus Valley were the people that developed the number system that is now universally used.

The Indus Valley people also developed the concept of zero. In their Sanskrit language, the word *zero* was *sunya*, it meant void or nothing.

The word *sunya* for void or nothing translated into Arabic was *sifr*, or cipher in English. One of the first mathematicians to write a book about this number system that is erroneously called arabic numbers was Leonardo of Pisa, Italy. He wrote the book on mathematics in 1202, and from his book chiefly the English spread the number system which is now used universally over the world. The book was written in Italian, and the Old Italian name for *sifr* or cipher was *zephirum* or *zepiro*. From the Old Italian word *zepiro*, it was adopted into the English language and became zero.

THE GREEKS WORKED GEOMETRY PROBLEMS, WROTE GEOMETRY BOOKS, BUT WERE WEAK IN ALGEBRA UNTIL DIOPHANTUS

A few uninformed have claimed that the Arabs developed the number system and algebra. Both of these ideas are preposterous for the people of the Indus Valley in northern Pakistan devised the world's number system, incorrectly referred to as arabic numbers, about 2500 BC.

In addition, algebraic operations were known by ancient Egyptians, Babylonians, and to Greeks at Alexandria. Truly, history reveals that Arabs or Ishmaelites did not invent our number system, or are there any historical records that prove that Ishmaelites invented algebra?

About two thousand years BC, when Abraham sired Isaac and Ishmael, Egyptians, Phoenicians, and ethnic Germanic people were in the Middle East. It is known that Phoenicians intermarried with other tribes, and it is preposterous to state that Germanic people did not comingle. Thus, on the basis that Ishmaelites were herdsmen and never left any record of intellectual achievements, it is most logical to credit the intellectual Arab composites with working algebra problems, not pure Ishmaelites.

Two famous Greek mathematicians that were very astute geometers and worked algebra were HERO (about 20—unknown) and DIOPHANTUS (20 AD-unknown.) Some historians speculate that Diophantus lived and worked at Alexandria, Egypt, at the same time as Hero, in the first century AD, while others speculate that Diophantus was born about two hundred years after Hero. Whichever is the case, Diophantus was an astute mathematician, and with his algebraic work, he was the first to treat fractions as numbers. Good fortune for history occurred when Diophantus recorded his algebraic work which, if not in the first century AD, was no later than the third century AD.

Thus, Egyptians and Babylonians preceded Diophantus in algebraic work, but Diophantus's work that was recorded established without any question the Greek genius working at Alexandria, Egypt, had brought algebraic operations to new mathematical level of excellence.

However, the work of Diophantus was improved upon by the French mathematician, DESCARTES, RENE (day-kahrt) (ra-nay) (1596-1650). It was Descartes that made great changes to algebraic operations. Descartes was the first to use letters at the beginning of the alphabet to denote constants and letters at the end of the alphabet to denote variables. In addition, he introduced the exponent and the square-root sign.

Therefore, Diophantus and Descartes were the mathematicians that brought algebra to a usable form in finding the value of unknowns. The false idea to credit Arabs with inventing algebra has been construed by falsely attributing its invention to the Muslim mathematical whiz, AL-KHWAROZMI—Muhammed ibn Musa (about 780-about 850) This mathematical whiz was an Uzbek (southern Russia) Muslim that gained immortality in the history of science of mathematics by extending the work of the Greek mathematician, DIOPHANTUS.

Al-Khwarozmi wrote an algebra book about seven hundred years after Diophantus wrote a book about algebraic operations. Al-Khwarozmi's book was titled *The Science of Transposition and Cancellation*. The Arabic word for "transposition" is *al-jabr*, and this is the root word for the English word algebra.

The Uzbek Al-Khwarozmi incorporated into his work the Sanskrit number system, including the zero, and drew heavily upon the algebraic work of Diophantus. In addition to the great probability of Al-Khwarozmi not being an Ishmaelite, he or any other Muslim DID NOT invent algebra.

TRUE HISTORICAL FACTS SHOULD BE HONORED

History has recorded a profound truth about the use of numbers. The astute mathematician DIOPHANTUS at Alexandria Egypt wrote a book about algebra over five hundred years before Mohammed was born and therefore before the cult of Islam was born. Persians, Greeks, and composites from intermarriage continued working with algebraic problems, and later descendants of the Etruscans in northern Italy worked with algebra problems. From there the Sanskrit number system and algebra were spread over the world by the English.

MOORS WERE SCIENTIFIC PEOPLE THAT BECAME EXTINCT

About 3000 BC, the land now known as Morocco had an influx of light-skinned, blue-eyed boat people. At that time, there were scattered throughout the land people with dark skin and black skin.

Later, Phoenicians immigrated to this region and intermarried with the descendents of the early settlers.

Several thousand years later, after Greece developed, some Greeks immigrated to the Moroccan region and intermarried with the merged Phoenicians and the early settlers. After the Romans developed, they named these light-skinned, blue-eyed people the Berbers.

Carthaginians were known to the Romans to be of Phoenician lineage, and the Roman word *Poeni* meant Phoenician. Thus, the English adjective *Punic* came from the Latin Punicus, and it was the Roman reference term for the Carthaginians. Thus, the Roman-Carthaginian wars in the first century BC are referred to as the Punic wars.

However, this region was still very diverse in racial mix, for there were and are equator people or tropical people with black skin and semitropical people that had lighter skin.

Thus, as the centuries passed, a composite people emerged consisting of the boat people that had been there for several thousand years, Phoenicians, and Greeks. The combined original Berbers that had intermarried with the Greeks and Phoenicians were a composite people and were referred to as Moors by the Spanish. The word *Moor* comes from the Spanish word *moro*; it is a word used to refer to any person of the Islamic belief.

After the Arabs conquered the land of the Moors in the seventh century, there was intermarriage with Arabs, and the Moors did accept the Muslim faith.

However, the intellectual Moors were not Arabs, they were a mixture of Berbers, Phoenicians, and Greeks. Yet, as time passed, more Arabs settled in the land of the Moors. This created a clash of cultures. Due to the fact that the Moors did not use strict regimens or self-discipline to preserve their culture, they slowly became absorbed by the Arabs and became extinct, as did the Egyptians from the influx of Nubian genes. Later, the Arabs occupied the land of Egypt, and the Egyptian culture became completely extinct. In addition, the Phoenicians, Etruscans, Greeks, and Romans became extinct for other reasons.

As the extinction force was changing the nature of the Moors, their proclivities for science and mathematics were waning, until the Moor character was superimposed by an Arab character. Therefore, the penchant for science and mathematics ceased.

Although, there exists a 1 percent of the intelligentsia in every tribe that are gifted, in the case of the Moors and every Muslim nation, adhering to Muslim doctrines prevented scientific advancement. Yet the fruits of the artisans are evident in mosques, though beautiful buildings for purposes of worship do not raise the standard of living for the masses.

SELF-DISCIPLINED PEOPLE ARE THE INVENTORS IN THE WORLD AND HAVE RAISED THE STANDARD OF LIVING IN NATIONS WHERE DISCIPLINE PREVAILS.

Since 1907 to 1997, there have been thirty-six Nobel Prizes awarded in the realms of science and mathematics to Jewish scientists and researchers. These Jewish Nobel Prize Laureates helped to bring forth our age of electronic wizardry while at the same time, NOT ONE Arabic Muslim has received a Nobel Prize.

If any of those Jewish Nobel Prize Laureates were in Israel, they would be a target for suicide bombers. In addition, Muslims believe that they go to heaven if they kill people such as Richard Rogers, Oscar Hammerstein, Benny Goodman, George Gershwin, Jerome Kern, Irving Berlin, Fritz Kreisler, Meredith Wilson, Leonard Bernstein, Andre Previn, and Barry Manilow, to name a few, plus the polio vaccine inventors, Jonas Salk and Albert Sabin.

ARABS ARE STILL A NONINVENTIVE PEOPLE.

If the world had to depend upon the Arabs to scientifically advance the world, advancement would cease. Their semideveloped nature is evident from the facts: Arabs do not honor the Nobel Prize committee, as they don't honor the world court at the Hague, Amnesty International, World Associations for the Advancement of Science, the Olympics, or the decision of the United Nations to create the state of Israel.

JEWS AND THE LAND OF ISRAEL

Jews have been returning to Jerusalem since about the year 1880. When they arrived in the Holy Land, they did not squat on land owned by someone. They bought the land.

On November 29, 1947, the United Nations began the legal work to make the enclave of Jewish people in the Holy Land a sovereign nation.

On May 14, 1948, Israel was officially recognized as a sovereign nation. The United Nations did allot a huge tract of desert to be added to the land of Israel. So at that time, the land of Israel was about 65 percent desert. In time, the Israelis developed the desert land and made it flower.

The day after Israel was officially recognized, May 15, 1948, Arab nations Egypt, Syria, Jordan, Iraq, and Lebanon declared war on Israel. Their purpose was to defeat Israel in warfare and eliminate the Israeli nation from the face of the earth.

Although the Arab nations had more money, millions of people, and seemed to be stronger militarily, the small nation of Israel, while only numbering about 806,000 people at that time, defeated the Arabs by using brains over brawn.

However, after the Arab defeat, the Arab nations did not concentrate on educating their people and developing with peaceful intents. The result was three more wars against Israel.

In 1967, the Arabs made their third war on the nation of Israel, and again, the Israelis defeated the Arab nations. Since recorded history, when two nations use war to settle their differences, the losing nation or nations have always lost all or some of their land. England, France, Spain, Germany, Japan lost land to the victors in wars.

In the 1967 war, among the Arab nations that attacked Israel were the Palestinians. When the six-day war was over, Israel occupied the land from the Mediterranean Sea to the west, the Jordan River to the east, Lebanon and Syria to the north and northeast, and Egypt to the south, including the Sinai Peninsula.

The Palestinian Arabs that live in the land of Israel lost their national identity in the 1967 war against Israel and are now squatters. They are permitted to live on Israeli land, if they live peacefully. The so-called Palestinians want to reclaim the land that they lost in the war against Israel just as the American Indians wanted to reclaim the land that they lost in warfare to the American colonists. However, as Native American Indians before them, these Arab people would rather engage in a guerilla war (however how long it takes) than submit and merge into the developing world in a peaceful manner.

However, in perhaps an unprecedented act in the history of mankind, the entire Sinai Peninsula that Egypt had lost to Israel in the 1967 war was returned to Egypt as a peace offering. But that did not quell the seething hatred and jealously in many Arab minds against Israelis, and further aggressive tactics, including suicide bombings, were planned by zealots to be committed in a continued war against Israel.

The idea to deceive any naive Muslim to be a "bombman" or suicide bomber was spawned about eight hundred years ago by a Muslim by the name of Hasan bin Sabbah. He culled poor young boys from poor environments and trained them to become sacrificial bombers of those that he wanted assassinated. He fed the boys and taught Islamic dogma to them. When they were made ready to be used in an assassination, he would give them hashish and bring prostitutes to their bed. After awakening in the morning, they were told to expect that type of "paradise" when they died for Allah in a suicide bombing. Bin Sabbah used these boys to assassinate sheiks, emirs, and any influential person that interfered with his own power struggles. The use of suicide bombers was not discontinued after the demise of bin Sabbah, but the civilized world did not hear of Muslim atrocities to their own people until 1983. In that year, a Muslim suicide bomber gained entry to the American embassy in Beirut and managed to kill sixty people. That marked the beginning of suicide bombings in modern times.

Six months after that bombing, the American and French military barracks in Beirut was bombed by a suicide bombing, and three hundred people were killed.

In 1993, the tactic was used in Israel when a suicide bomber now referred to as a Shahid drove a van filled with explosive gas cylinders into a crowded area. His attempt at mass killing was not as effective as the terrorists planned, for instead of killing scores of Israelis, only eight were injured.

After this 1993 terrorist attack upon Israelis, a procurement program was established to buy explosives, ball bearings, and nails from Christian nations to make bombs. Then a training program was begun by Muslims that had been educated in a Christian nation to train suicide bombers for this type of warfare.

A promise of rewards from Allah after the suicide bomber's demise was given to the naïve. They were and are promised virgins for their sexual pleasure, and this has a gripping power on their deceived minds.

JEALOUSLY OF JEWISH ACCOMPLISHMENTS FUELED THEIR HATRED.

The Arab jealously and envy of the Jewish sociocultural system generated into seething hatred. The leaders of the Arabs that live on land now owned by the Israelis began to train their youth from a very early age to hate Israeli people. Pictures of dead suicide bombers were posted in places where those that are called Palestinians could readily see. These so-called martyrs became role models for the youth. By the time a child becomes three years old, they are taught to recite mind-conditioning verses that prepare them to become a suicide bomber. In children's early schools, they are taught to march in military style while chanting hate slogans against Israelis.

The theme of hatred toward Israelis on radio and TV programs is used in a manner that exceeds the training camps of Adolph Hitler. Even comic books are used to teach hatred against Israelis. The desire to die a kamikaze death is stronger than that of young Japanese that were deceived to die a suicide death for the emperor and the warlords during the last of WWII. With eager suicide bombers to use, the zealots formed more terrorist organizations. Not all Arabs belong to these terrorist groups, but almost all Arabs are sympathetic to their causes. They are bound together by their Muslim faith. Any Muslim that criticizes the Koran would be marked for death by a Muslim cleric. This fanatical devotion to Islam was seen when Palestinians were seen clapping their hands in streets when the American Twin Towers were bombed by a kamikaze attack on September, 11, 2001.

At any time, the nonviolent Muslims could hunt down and kill the extremists, and peace would prevail, but Muslims will not kill other Muslims (excepting in their own tribal wars) even for their own peace and security. Therefore, in a very clannish manner, Muslims will live together and will die together.

Compounding this emotional and unstable nature of Muslim zealots is the fact that all adherents to their faith firmly believe their faith and culture is mandated by God and believe that God will reward th'em for killing non-Muslims. This conviction is responsible for creating a low moral conscience.

DON'T GO INTO THE JUNGLE WHERE WILD ANIMALS LIVE

This fact is continually revealed by Muslims' heinous murders of Christians, Jews, and Hindus.

In 2002, a reporter for the *Wall Street Journal* whose name is known by almost all Americans, Daniel Perl, was tricked by seemingly friendly Muslims to be driven to a place for an interview. After arriving at a Muslim meeting place, he was bound, and then on January 31, 2002, he was beheaded. The gruesome act was videotaped and later shown on an Islamic TV station.

GRUESOME AND *GHASTLY* ARE WORDS THAT FALL SHORT IN DESCRIBING THE BARBARITY.

Two other horrific cases of murder that testify to this fact occurred in the Philippines and Indonesia on August 22, 2002. Reuters reported two grisly murders too gruesome to comprehend by civilized people that were committed by Philippine Muslims. Among the news briefs from Reuters was the following story.

> Muslim guerrillas in the Philippines have beheaded two Christian preachers . . . Officials said the heads were found on Thursday wrapped in plastic in the main town of Patikul on southern Jolo island, two days after the Abu Sayyaf seized the two male preachers and six other hostages. One head was in a fruit stall in a public market.
>
> "This is what will happen to those who do not believe in Allah. This is part of our jihad" (holy war), said a note found near one of

the heads of the preachers who were Filipinos from the Christian-dominated mainland city of Zamboanga.

In May 2004, a video was shown on an Islamic Web site about a beheading of an American in Iraq. Five Muslim men wearing headscarves and black ski masks were shown with a man bound and wearing an orange jumpsuit. The Muslims were standing over the American in preparation for execution, Muslim style—beheading. The gruesome act was videotaped, and the American's head was held in front of the camera. They obeyed the directives of the Koran and firmly believed that Allah would reward them someday for the murders.

THREE SCHOOLGIRLS WERE BEHEADED IN INDONESIA.

Three grisly murders occurred on October 29, 2005, in Indonesia. In this situation, a group of high school girls were walking to a private Christian school when they were attacked by unidentified attackers, later caught and tried for the murders.

The three girls were beheaded, and a fourth was seriously injured. In a Cro-Magnon act of brutality, the girl's heads were carried away and disposed of about a mile distant.

Behavior that can be associated to the Cro-Magnon days is an accurate appraisal. However, when all peoples that are not Muslims consider the fact that the Koran directs Muslims to cut off the heads of infidels and cut off their fingertips, it is very clear that a type of mental derangement has a grip on Muslims.

A FEW MUSLIM NATIONS ARE TRYING TO ADVANCE

Interspersed through the Middle East are people that are not pure Ishmaelites. These composites, as given, are partly English and other ethnic mixtures and are very different from the more pure Ishmaelites. Some of the intelligentsia of this group have studied in Christian nations and have adopted into their nation some of these democratic nations' sociocultural lifestyles. Two examples of this modernization are Qatar and Bahrain. These nations have adopted a type of Reformed Islam and are striving to adapt to the modern world.

However, being naive about the pitfalls of an open society, some hedonism is creeping into their emerging Reformed Islam. Without disciplined growth, these nations could degenerate into societies where gambling, topless bars, belly dancing, whoredom, and the accompanying increases of crime will surely destroy their culture. Conservative Muslims and Wahhabi Muslim nations view the two nations mentioned as outcasts.

Another long practiced cultural tradition of Wahhabi (fundamentalist) Muslims that is also a factor in retarding their development is the practice of polygamy and treating women as a subclass. However, the Persian Gulf nations of Qatar and Bahrain are rapidly becoming modernized, and the practice of women being forced to wear a burka to keep their faces covered is becoming outmoded.

THE NATURE OF ARABS OR ISHMAELITES IS GREATLY INFLUENCED BY THEIR PHILOSOPHIC BELIEFS.

THE PHILOSOPHY OF ISLAM HAS NOT ONLY PREVENTED ARABS FROM PERSONAL DEVELOPMENT, IT HAS ALSO PREVENTED ARAB NATIONS FROM ASSISTING IN HUMANITY'S DEVELOPMENT.

While the education process in every civilized nation concentrates on every branch of science and the humanities teach behavior conducive to good mental health,

MUSLIMS ARE ORDERED TO KILL JEWS, KILL CHRISTIANS, and KILL HINDUS.

IF MUSLIMS ARE CRITICIZED FOR THEIR HEINOUS DEEDS, THEY RIOT AND ASSASSINATE GOOD PEOPLE IN THE WORLD.

The regimens for self-discipline and self-improvement are not directives in their Koran.

HATRED OF AND VIOLENCE TOWARD JEWS IS PREVALENT IN EVERY MUSLIM LAND.

Iran, once Persia, and the land of the Aryans, now has Arabs in their ethnic mix. Iran now stands foremost as the greatest terrorist nation in the world. The genetic lineage of the Persians and Aryans in Iran has enabled the present day Iranians to be superior to other Muslim nations. However, these composite people have adopted Islam, and now Iran manufactures implements of war, has a weapons-of-mass-destruction program, and has equipped the Hezbollah solely for the purpose of killing Jews.

Since the invasion of the Muslim nation Iraq, the hearts of Iranian leaders has become darker with hatred. They are responsible for an increase of evil spreading throughout Iraq.

THROUGH THEIR DISTORTED VIEW OF REALITY, THE IRANIANS BELIEVE THAT ALLAH WOULD SAVE THEM FROM ANY MILITARY RETALIATION BECAUSE THEY BELIEVE THAT ISLAM IS THE ONLY TRUE RELIGION.

It is time to put their ideas to an in-depth analysis.

Using an ideology to wreak havoc on the world in the name of a religion needs to be addressed.

RELIGION DEFINED

RELIGION is a term used to define MAN'S psychological or spiritual status about his origin and ultimate destiny.

RELIGION is an Anglicized or English word from the Greek root word *religion*, meaning piety (devotion to religion), and the meaning of the root word *religare* means to bind back, to bind together, therefore to bind back to God, to bind together with God. Its further definition given in *Webster's Unabridged Dictionary*:

1. a belief in divine supernatural powers to be obeyed and worshipped as the creator(s) ruler(s) of creation. (in Christianity this is God the father, the Holy Ghost and the Son Lord Jesus the Christ) 2. an expression of this belief by personal conduct and ritual. 4. a state of mind or way of life expressing love for and trust in God, and one's will and effort to act according to the will of God.

2. Thus, my definition for RELIGION within the context of these respected definitions is: a personal effort to love, honor, respect, and worship a divine creator (God) with order and systemized routines to establish a binding together of the devotee with God, to set before all mankind a lifestyle that is exemplary. (After order and systemized routines are defined, this definition precludes any form of "insane permissiveness" and defines RELIGION with responsibility.)

3. If Americans could succeed in making this a legal definition, it would disallow students from interrupting order in a secular classroom with their personal wrinkle of worship and would preclude worshippers from (any number of worshippers using RELIGION as a weapon against others to interfere with American systemized business and travel, i.e. praying in the middle of streets i.e. at Times Square at any time).

4. Webster may also have incorrectly honored the fact that our language is changing, for a corrupted meaning of RELIGION is given as meaning whatever a person deems to worship. Crazy person, deranged, or perverted, it makes no difference—the object can be worshipped and is their RELIGION. I quote from Webster: "humanism is his religion."

5. All RELIGIONS have nothing to do with ANY conduct counter to the rules of "good mental health," and within the context of "humanism is his religion," our source for word definition as given by semanticists did confuse RELIGION with philosophy.

6. PHILOSOPHY, defined from its ambiguous definition where its meaning can be confused with religion, is as follows: the general beliefs, concepts, and attitudes of an individual or group.

7. Common sense or very elemental reasoning reveals that Islam is NOT a religion. Common sense or very elemental reasoning also reveals that Islam is a philosophy. In addition, the Christian Bible states plainly that a philosophy is NOT a religion.

8. (Col 2:8, KJV) "Beware lest any man spoil you through philosophy and vain deceit, after the tradition of men, after the rudiments of the world, and not after Christ."

9. Therefore, by defining the word *religion*, Islam is NOT a religion. Islam is a philosophy.

In America, the FIRST AMENDMENT in the Constitution, grants freedom of RELIGION. It does not grant freedom of philosophies.

However, whether Islam is a religion or a philosophy, Muslims have a right to practice their beliefs and adhere to their culture in their own countries.

TRYING TO RULE THE WORLD FROM WASHINGTON IS THE REASON FOR THE MUSLIM BACKLASH.

More pain, misery, and agony has been forced upon the peoples of the world by the self-styled "Caesars" in Washington than the terrorist attacks by the Muslims.

If the Washington "Self-Styled Caesars" would not have waged war, interfered in the national affairs of Spain (and later Cuba and the Philippines, then Cuba again by deposing Batista and providing a way for Castro to came to power), Vietnam, Korea, and China, Cuba (again, which resulted in the Missile Crisis), Somalia, the Russia—Afghanistan conflict and the Yugoslavian civil war, our world would be different, and all of God's people would be further advanced in our developmental trek. The Law of Recompense will balance all of these offenses and interventions into the affairs of other developing nations. Caesar exploits must stop for the well-being of America and the world in general.

The mind forces that shape the future of America have created a chaotic and divisive future from past abuses to others. Only truthful and fervent prayer can alleviate the consequences that are here and escalating. Pray and pray diligently for forgiveness and restructure our government to prevent "political gangsters" and self-styled "Caesars" from bringing havoc upon our nation.

Interacting with Muslims on a personal level has had and will have, if continued, a weakening and destructive affect upon the American psyche.

America, England, France, and Germany have permitted Muslims to immigrate to their nations and must now bear the consequences of their foolish policies.

Only Muslims and those deluded would believe that America, England, Germany, and France are blessed with good fortunes from allowing Muslims into their lands.

After the World Trade Center and Pentagon bombings, President Bush should have asked for and used war powers to deport every Muslim that came into America since 1980, excepting those of the intelligentsia that are professionals, are married, have children, and could convince immigration officials in an interview that they pose no threat to America. In addition, the immigration doors should have been closed to all Muslims. The idea held within an evil philosophy, a so-called religion, to destroy America and destroy all that are not Muslims is a personal matter for Muslims.

TRUTH IS NOT ELUSIVE

Giving Washington extreme liberals the power to permit avowed enemies to enter America illustrates strongly that some of our enemies are in our own federal government.

Allowing Muslims to stay in America and taxing the American people to maintain surveillance is a twisted or distorted sense of freedom and more resembles an act of war by our own government against the American people.

The Law of Recompense takes the line of least resistance, as is the nature of all energy, and the attraction to America for recompense from its terrible deeds to others attracted a people that had great glee at killing non-Muslims.

While Muslims are blamed for our problems, our real enemies have been and are the interlopers in Washington.

The following data concerning terrorist actions and assassinations reveals the treacherous nature of Muslims. In addition, it reveals that civilian Americans plus American embassies and military barracks were targets for murder and destruction. The fact that Norway, Sweden, Denmark, Netherlands, Germany, England, Canada, Australia, France, Belgium, Luxemburg, and Italy were not targets for terrorism deserves to be honestly explained. England's subway and bus bombings did not occur until after England engaged in the invasion of a Muslim nation, Iraq.

Only America was trying to change the culture of Islam. Only America was trying to change the political structure of Muslim nations. Only America used its military arsenal to interfere into the internal affairs of Muslim nations.

Powerful groups in Muslim nations have stated plainly, "We do not want a Christian nation to be occupiers in our nation." They have said: "GET OUT." When political leaders that can be psychologized as arrogant self-styled "Caesars" ignore the will of Muslim people, the results can be predicted. Extremist groups within a Muslim nation have stated plainly, "WE DECLARE WAR ON YOU."

Many times, a naïve-seeming "do-gooder" tried to interfere in a family squabble that was loud and boisterous only to have the entire family TURN ON THE INTERLOPER.

AMERICA CAN STILL BE A LAND WHERE WEALTH FLOWS AS MILK AND HONEY.

I repeat again, if a national referendum is needed, then so be it. America must curtail "Caesar exploits" and establish a balanced budget amendment with a punishment proviso for federally elected politicians to forfeit a year's salary if the yearly federal budget is not balanced. Also, "buccaneering capitalists" and "political gangsters" should not thwart my great gift to the American people.

MUSLIM ATTACKS ON NON-MUSLIMS FOLLOWS

I have not been able to record all the Muslim attacks on non-Muslims. Some attacks do not reach the media, and my research is conducted by myself with no staff to assist.

1968 June 5—Bobby Kennedy assassinated by an Arab.

1972 September 5—Eleven Israelis murdered at the Munich Olympics by Arabs.

1973—Oil Embargo began October 19 and 20 and continued until March 18, 1974.
   In civilized industrial nations, cartels, price fixing, and monopolies have been outlawed to protect the general public against blatant buccaneering capitalism. But in semideveloped nations where traces of primitive traits still exist and a quick-to-warring mentality exists, business is conducted with a buccaneering attitude, and "let the buyer beware" prevails. Also, trade is used as a weapon whenever the situation enables business practices to be manipulated for weapons. Arabs did not and do not have the mentality to drill for oil, build oil-storage complexes and refining plants, but when civilized nations did develop the means to capitalize on the oil resources, the Arabs confiscated the developed oil industry by using a communistic or socialistic tactic called nationalizing.

1981 May 13—Catholic Pope John Paul II nearly assassinated by an Arab.

1981 October 6—President of Egypt Anwar al-Sadat was assassinated by jihad-crazed Arab terrorists. The ringleader, Aman al-Zawahri, later joined the Osama bin Laden terrorist organization. The assassination of Sadat is another example of how black-hearted Muslims can be. When Sadat was elected president of Egypt, he freed hundreds of Muslims that belonged to the extremist Egyptian "Muslim Brotherhood." Some of those freed assassinated the very man that had set them free from prison. Others formed new radical groups that were determined to establish a fundamental Islam government throughout other Arab nations, and of these groups formed were the "Egyptian Islamic Jihad," the "Islamic Group," and terrorist groups in other nations, including Hamas.

1983 April 18—U.S. embassy bombed in Beirut. Sixty-three were killed, among those were seventeen Americans.

1983 October 23—Marine barracks bombed in Beirut. Two hundred forty-one American servicemen killed.

1984 September 20—U.S. embassy annex in Beirut bombed. Sixteen people killed.

1985—Kidnappings of British, French, and Americans begun in Beirut. Terry Anderson, an AP bureau chief, was kidnapped in March 1985 and held for 2,454 days until released in December 1991. Two kidnapped victims were killed: William Buckley and William Higgins. Others kidnapped were Reverend Lawrence Jenco, university officials David Jacobson and Thomas Southerland, plus Peter Kilburn, Joseph Cicippio, Terry Waite, and Edward Tracy.

1985 June 14—TWA Flight number 847 was hijacked by two Arabs in Athens, Greece. An American navy serviceman on board was beaten to death, and when the plane was forced to land in Beirut, his body was thrown from the plane to the ground.

1985 October 7—Cruise ship *Achille Lauro* was captured by Arabs. One American, Leon Klinghofer, was killed by pushing him with his wheelchair into the ocean.

1985 November 24—Palestinians Muslims hijacked an Egyptian jetliner that was parked at an airfield in Malta. Egyptian commandoes stormed the plane in a raid that killed fifty-eight people on the plane and two on the ground.

1986—German discotheque was bombed with a hand grenade by Arabs with a Syrian connection. Three were killed, two American servicemen died, and two hundred injured. In November 2001, a German court found four guilty of the 1986 German disco bombing, but the judge stated that the charge that Gadhafi or Gaddafi ordered the bombing was NOT proven (more about this later.)

1986 April—President Reagan commits huge blunder by ordering Libya bombed in retaliation to the discotheque bombing. Libya bombed in error, Khadafy's daughter killed in the American bombing.

1988 December 21—Airline Flight number 103 sabotaged by a bomb which exploded while the plane was over Lockerbie, Scotland. Two hundred fifty-nine were killed on the plane plus eleven on the ground. The bombing was speculated to be in retaliation to President Reagan's errant April 1986 bombing of Libya when Gaddafi's daughter was killed. This speculation is not an idle thought, for if the errant bombing of Libya had not occurred and Gaddafi's daughter had not been killed, most assuredly no plane would have been sabotaged.

1990 November 5—Rabbi Meir Kahane assassinated in New York. The accused assassin, el-Said-Nosair, an Arab Egyptian immigrant that fled the scene, also shot a man in the leg as he fled. He was accused of the murder but was acquitted and found guilty and sentenced to twenty-two years for illegal gun possession. The results of the trial is another case of the changing justice in America as was: the "jackpot" justice when GM was zapped 4.9 billion dollars to compensate six people for their injuries due to the excessive speed of a drunk driver, the murder of O. J. Simpson's wife and her companion, the murder of the Rabbi Yankel Rosenblum, the approval of perjury by the U.S. Senate in regard to Chief Executive Bill Clinton's perjury to the grand jury.

1991—In compliance to the anti-Christ movement, the American House of Representatives invited a Muslim, one of the most virulent enemies of Christianity and Judaism, to give an opening prayer at a session. The Supreme Court had already ruled that the United States was a Christian nation, and all legal documents are signed "In The Year of Our Lord," yet an avowed sly enemy to the United States was invited to the House of Representatives to offer a prayer. This was high mockery to God to invite an avowed "anti-Christ" person to pray in the highest lawmaking house in America. In 1999, this same Muslim was invited as an official guest at the U.S. State Department to commemorate a Muslim revered day. After the Twin Towers were attacked the first time in 1993, a list of Muslim enemies to America was published. This Muslim cleric, Iman Siraj Wahhaj, boasted in a Muslim speech that he had dinner with Secretary of State Madeline Albright after the list was published.

I try to fathom in depth the meaning of every event, and inviting an avowed enemy to be honored in government highest places only "makes sense" when the supposed servants of the people are actually "enemies of the people." Later, in a speech, Imam Wahhaj stated that democracy will fall and an Islamic government will replace democracy and invited all Americans to embrace Islam. In 2003, Imam Wahhaj was arrested for raising money for terrorists.

1993 February 26—First bombing of the World Trade Building by Arabs. Six people killed, more than a thousand injured.

1994—Hijacking a plane in an attempt to use it as a flying bomb first occurred in France. A member of the Armed Islamic Group, or GIA, hijacked an Air France Airbus jet. The hijacker intended to crash the plane into the center of Paris, but French commandoes of Marseilles stormed the plane before the suicide mission got off the ground.

1994 December 11—Ramzi (Ramsey) Yousef, also known in Wales as Abdul Basit, was trained in bomb making in Afghanistan. He planted a bomb on a plane in Manila that was discovered before the plane was airborne. It was one of the most sophisticated bombs in comparison to the bomb that brought down the airline flight number 103 that was sabotaged by a bomb which exploded while the plane was over Lockerbie, Scotland, killing 270 people.

Yousef escaped and later returned to Manila in 1995 to plan a suicide attack on the pope.

1994 December—A Philippine Airlines flight to Japan had a bomb planted on it that exploded and killed one passenger and injured six more. It ripped a hole in the floor but did not down the plane.

1995 November 13—Seven people, including five Americans, killed when two bombs explode at the OPM-SANG building in Riyadh, Saudi Arabia.

1995—During the pope's January 11 to January 21 Asian visits, Arabs plotted to kill the pope with a suicide bomber in Manila. The chemicals they were preparing in a hotel room caught fire, and they were caught. Ramsey Yousef (phonetic spelling) was the mastermind behind the plot and was also a mastermind behind the first bombing of the NY Twin Towers. He again escaped from Manila but was later caught, brought to America, was tried, convicted, and was sent to prison for his part in the first Twin Towers bombing.

1996 June 25—Followers of bin Laden detonate a bomb at U.S. military base near Dhahran, Saudi Arabia, killing nineteen American soldiers and wounding hundreds of Americans and Saudi Arabians.

1996 January—Muslims in New York conspire to bomb bridges and tunnels. A leading inciter to these destructive schemes was a blind Egyptian Muslim cleric by the name of Omar Sheik Abdel Rahman. He was sentenced to life imprisonment for seditious conspiracy. A son of his became a member of bin Laden's terrorist organization and planned to hijack a plane and demand that his father be sent free or he would use the plane to crash into buildings. Fortunately, he was caught in Afghanistan during the search for terrorists, and the plan was never executed.

1996 June 25—Khobar Towers in Arabia bombed with a truck bomb. Nineteen killed.

1998 December—U.S. embassies in Nairobi, Kenya, and Dar es Salaam, Tanzania bombed by Muslims. Two hundred fifty-two killed, including twelve Americans. Five tbhousand injured.

1999 October 31—An Arab copilot in Egypt Air flight 900 crashed the plane into the sea, killing 217 people. Since the fight for Okinawa at the close of WW II, this was only the second time that a pilot turned kamikaze, seized a plane, and used it as a weapon for mass destruction. The other time an emotionally unstable pilot attempted to seize a plane was on October 7, 1994. This attempt to seize a plane and turn it into a flying bomb was committed by a Federal Express Negro or Afro-American pilot. An off-duty Negro pilot hitched a ride on a Fed Ex plane and attacked the crew with a hammer and speargun. He wanted to crash the plane into a Fed Ex building, but the crew subdued him even after they received near-fatal injuries from being beaten by a hammer. The pilot of the plane was so badly injured that he never was able to pilot another plane for Fed Ex.

1999 December—Arab radical from Algeria caught as he was trying to illegally enter the United States from Canada while on his way to bomb the LA airport.

2000 October 12—Navy destroyer USS *Cole* was bombed by one or more Arab suicide bombers at a Yemen port in the Persian Gulf. Seventeen American servicemen killed.

2001 January 25—A cabinet-level meeting on terrorism issues was sought by Richard Clarke. He was rebuffed by the Bush administration and was told to work through committees at a lower level. Bush's craving to get Saddam was the top priority at any cost to Americans even at a lax focus on terrorism. This proved to be a costly and stupid mistake.

2001 September 11—Four American passenger planes were hijacked by nineteen Arabs in a well-planned scheme to use the planes as flying bombs. Two planes were crashed into the New York World Trade Building—Twin Towers. One was crashed into the Pentagon Building in D.C., and some gallant American passengers overtook United Flight number 175, and the plane crashed in an open field in Somerset County, southeast of Pittsburgh, Pennsylvania. That plane was headed towards Washington, D.C., and was only a half-hour away when the plane crashed. Over 3,000 people were killed in the combined terrorist attacks on September 9, 2001.

More people were killed from New York in the tower buildings than the total amount of people that were killed in the attack on Pearl Harbor. The exact number of deaths in the Twin Towers destruction has been calculated to be 2,749 killed and missing. Of that number, 800 bodies were burned to powder and never found. Only about 1,500 people were identified.

After the attacks, Osama bin Laden stated that Israelis and Americans will be targeted and asked all Pakistanis to commit themselves to a holy war (jihad) against the United States and Israel.

2001 September 11—Condoleeza Rice was scheduled to give a speech but canceled after the Twin Tower attacks. She and Colin Powell were already convinced by President Bush that Saddam Hussein had WMD, and Iraq had to be invaded. President had longed to be president as early as 1999 and longed to depose Saddam Hussein. However, after becoming president, deposing Saddam was viewed by the CIA as next to impossible. The only option left was war against Iraq. This too seemed to be an untenable project. According to Bob Woodward in his book, *Plan of Attack*, he states the idea of accusing Saddam Hussein of having weapons of mass destruction was "dreamed up" by Dick Cheney. This then became the theme in public relations. President

Bush began a public relations program that continually accused Saddam of having weapons of mass destruction.

Therefore, after the Twin Towers attacks on September 11, 2001, the proposed speech by Condoleeza Rice was cancelled.

Her proposed speech was formulated from Dick Cheney's basic ideas—that Saddam Hussein had weapons of mass destruction. The warnings given by Richard Clarke about terrorist attacks against America were ignored in her proposed speech, and the focus was shifted to missile defense.

This is another strong case against many of President Bush's inner circle that were deceived to ignore terrorist threats and focus on invading Iraq to gain political popularity as Reagan before.

2001 October 6, Saturday—Khobar, Arabia. A bomb exploded at a place non-Arabs or foreigners frequent. An American and an Englishman were killed. Several were wounded.

2001 October 5—Boca Raton, Florida. The first terrorist attack against America using an organic, biological chemical—anthrax germs. Putting anthrax germs in letters and mailing the letters to the target person carried out the attack. The perpetrator was never apprehended. America used tons of an inorganic chemical on the Vietnamese land that later caused 500,000 birth defects to newborn children. An international team of scientists blamed the exceedingly high number of birth defects on the American chemical, AGENT ORANGE.

The Law of Recompense has not been balanced from America's military interference in the Vietnam and Korean affairs, and the brew of hatred toward the United States is fomenting.

2002 May 11—The French assistance to enable Pakistani submarines to launch nuclear missiles was revealed to the world when in Karachi a car bomb killed eleven French naval engineers that were working on a nuclear launching system for a Pakistani submarine. The French sold Exocet missiles to Argentina that were used against England in the Falkland Island war, and now were eager and willing to equip Pakistan with a submarine nuclear launching capability. It seems as though the French have forgotten how Americans died on the Normandy beaches to free them from Nazi occupation. If America ever is bombed by Arabs that were enabled by France, it should be known until the end time of man that France supplied the weapons and due to this has also become a rogue nation and an enemy of the United States.

2001 December 13—A squad of five Muslim suicide attackers from Pakistan attacked the Indian parliament building, killing seven security guards and a gardener on what I believe to be a diversionary tactic engineered by Osama bin Laden to take the focus from the intense search for him in Afghanistan. The diversion was probably successful because it was later stated by American intelligence that bin Laden had escaped and was probably in Pakistan. The possibility of an Osama bin Laden-engineered coup in Pakistan to get control of the atomic bombs now increases and becomes very, very ominous.

2001 December 22—An English national that had joined a Muslim extremist group in England by the name of Richard C. Reid tried to set off an explosive device in his shoe on an American Airlines Flight 63 that was bound for Miami from Paris.

He had bought a one-way ticket from Paris to Miami, had no luggage, and did not appear to be a traveler. He had some facial hair, long hair that was tied in a ponytail, and generally did not have a tidy appearance. American Airlines people refused to allow him on board because of his profile that fitted a terrorist. The next day, French authorities gave approval for him to board the plane. While in flight, a stewardess caught him trying to light a fuse that protruded from his sneaker. She hollered for help, and several male passengers subdued him. The plane's captain diverted from Miami to Boston where he was arrested when the plane landed.

After the explosive device was examined by the FBI, it was determined that Richard Reid did not contrive the device since his intelligence level would not have enabled him to contrive the sophisticated bomb. It was also of the type that was used on the flight over Lockerbie, Scotland, and set in a plane in Manila by Ramsey Yousef.

2002 January 2—Twentieth hijacker indicted. The four planes that were hijacked on September 11 had five hijackers on the plane except for United Flight Number 175 that was overtaken by some gallant American passengers, and the plane crashed in an open field in Somerset County, southeast of Pittsburgh, Pennsylvania. That plane had four hijackers.

A Muslim that was detained by the immigration service by the name of Zacarias Moussaoui had left a trail in the US exactly as the nineteen hijackers had left, and his actions strongly suggested that he was to be the twentieth hijacker. Prior to September 11, Richard Reid had telephoned Moussaoui from London. While no man is talking, a link to bin Laden's al-Qaeda terrorist organization on the basis of their psychological profile is convincing.

2002 January 23—the bureau chief for the *Wall Street Journal* in Southeast Asia, Daniel Perl, (son of the scientist Martin L. Perl, a 1995 Nobel Prize laureate) was kidnapped in Karachi, Pakistan, by Arab terrorists and killed several weeks later. Journalist Daniel Perl was investigating the activities of Richard Reid, whose near-terrorist act was to blow up an airplane with a shoe bomb. Pictures of the captured journalist were circulated, and news of his death was revealed before February 21. Therefore, he was killed before February 21st.

2002 July 31—Five Americans were killed and four wounded by a Hamas-engineered bombing at the Hebrew University in Israel. A total of eighty were wounded, and in addition to the five Americans killed, two Israelis were also killed. There have been dozens of car bombs, truck bombs, and suicide bombings in Israel that have been committed by war-crazed Muslim lunatics.

The kidnappers and killers of Daniel Perl were sought with vigor by authorities, including American investigators, although the five Americans that were killed by the Hamas-engineered bombing in the Israel University seemed to be received by the G. W. Bush Administration with faint interest. Instead, the revengeful idea to attack Iraq was the key topic at the White House because, as President Bush stated, "Hussein tried to kill my dad." Finding a way to justify an invasion of Iraq was the behind-the-scenes topic at the White House since early in 2001.

2002 October 7—Two Muslim terrorists that had ties to al-Qaeda killed a United States marine on the Kuwaiti Island, Failaka, in the Persian Gulf.

INDONESIAN BOMBINGS

2000 August 1—a bomb injures the Philippine ambassador to Indonesia and kills two people.

2000 September 13—Jakarta Stock Exchange building bombed by a car bomb in the garage. Two killed, sixteen injured.

2002 December 25—Eleven Christian churches bombed on Christmas Eve, killing nineteen and injuring about a hundred.

2002 October 12—On Kula Beach on the isle of Bali, a small vacation haven for tourists was rocked by a backpack suicide bomber and a bomb in a Mitsubishi van that was set off by remote control. It killed 187 and injured 189 people, mostly Australians. Some bodies were never found. Among those killed were five Americans. An Islamic group that goes by the name Jemaah Islamiyah is suspected of the terrorist act. Its leader, Mr. Abu Bakar, was arrested and is suspected to also have been involved in Christian church bombing two years prior that killed 19 people.

2003 August 5—Marriott Hotel in South Jakarta was bombed by a suicide car bomb. Twelve people killed, 150 injured.

2004 September 9—In Jakarta, at the Australian embassy, a suicide car bomber kills three and injures eleven.

2005 May 28—In a crowded market located in a Christian enclave, two bombs explode, killing about twenty-two and injuring forty.

2005 October 1—On the island of Bali again, three crowded restaurants were bombed, killing about twenty-five and injuring about a hundred.

Ah yes! Very deranged people. They believe that God rewards them for killing innocent people by supplying them with virgins for sexual escapades.

2002 October 24—Fifty-four Muslim terrorists seized a Russian theater that was featuring the Russian musical *Nord-Ost*. There were 750 attendees watching the play. Seventy-five were foreign. Two were Americans.

Two days later, on Saturday, the twenty-sixth, Russian Special Forces gassed the theater with a debilitating gas then stormed the theater, killing fifty of the terrorists. Some theater patrons died from the gas. The two Americans were treated at a hospital and lived.

2002 October 28—An American administrator, Laurence Foley, stationed in Amman, Jordan, was shot three times in the chest as he was about to get into his car at his residence. A Jordanian Islamic terrorist group claimed responsibility.

2002 November 28—A hotel in Mombasa, Kenya, was bombed while about the same time two SAM missiles were shot and narrowly missed a civilian Boeing 757 civilian passenger plane as it took off from the Mombasa Airport. The plane carried 261 passengers and the crew. The hotel bombing killed twelve people, including one American, and injured eighty people. This is the first known al-Qaeda terrorist attack against Israelis.

2002 December 9—A North Korean ship, the *So San*, with fifteen Scud missiles concealed under tons of cement, was intercepted in the Indian Ocean. The ship was tracked by satellite as it left Korea and was illegally flying a flag of Cambodia. Scud missiles can be used as weapons of mass destruction by arming them with biological or chemical warheads. The Scuds were actually a purchase of the Yemen government in violation of a promise given several weeks prior that it would not buy Scuds.

This international event reveals a deeper threat that North Korea poses.

Only one Scud missile armed with bacteria or nerve gas fired over New York from a freighter could kill several million people. Yet while Scuds pose a very dangerous situation to American facilities worldwide and the American homeland, North Korea's intention to build atomic bombs is a far more ominous condition. It is no longer just an intention, for on October 8, 2006, North Korea detonated a small nuclear device. The fact that is alarming about North Korea's missile arsenal is the fact that they intend to sell atomic bombs. The Korean mess was created by "self-styled" Caesars in Washington and was begun by the Truman administration. (Just a police action, according to Harry Truman.)

2002 December 30—Three American missionaries were killed and one wounded in Yemen by a thirty-year-old Arab by the name of Abed Abdul Razak Kamel. The three killed were William E. Koehn (60) from Arlington, Texas; Dr. Martha C. Myers (57) from Montgomery, Alabama; Kathleen A. Gariety (53) Wauwatosa, Wisconsin; and the injured man was Donald W. Caswell (49) Levelland, Texas. The Muslim confessed for the motive for the attack. He said they were teaching Christianity. Other Americans that are killed by Arabs were not teaching Christianity. The truth is very clear. The citizens in many Muslim nations overwhelmingly do not want Americans in their country.

FREEDOM OF CHOICE IN A DEMOCRATIC NATION

Since American politicians brag about America being a democratic nation, would the "Devil Driven" Washington politicians honor a referendum vote if the people of a Muslim nation would vote to have Americans barred from their nation? Not likely. American politicians crave to play the role "Caesars" and to do the will of and favor "special interest groups," not the will of the vast majority. The "Caesars" want to rule the world from Washington. The servants of the "Prince of Darkness" are eager to create a semblance of a democracy as a tool to serve "special interest groups."

The next Muslim or Arab act of aiding and abetting terrorist causes is not in chronological order. The following is a case that was brought to the attention of the general public by a writer for the *Wall Street Journal*. The heading for the article states

"Muslim FBI Agent Is Accused Of Not Taping Terror Suspects"
By Glenn R. Simpson.

On two occasions, a Muslim FBI agent by the name of Gamal Abdel-Hafiz was assigned to investigate Muslims in America that were suspected of collecting funds to funnel them to terrorist organizations that were headquartered in Muslim nations. On both occasions, he was instructed to wear a recording device to record the fine details of the scheme. On both occasions, the Muslim FBI agent refused to record the conversation on the grounds that a Muslim does not record another Muslim. The insubordination began in 1999 and occurred again a year later.

This is another case where suspected enemies used American laws to continue to plan destructive acts against America, for this Muslim claimed that he was being discriminated against. If you ask any security-conscious American what happened to the Muslim, a not-surprising answer would probably be that HE WAS FIRED. That would be natural for a grievous act of insubordination, but in fact, he was reassigned to Arabia. My question comes from the knowledge of Muslim doctrine. Why was a person that belongs to an evil philosophy that is founded on the idea to kill infidels and use violence to subjugate all non-Muslims ever allowed to become an FBI man? There is no logical pro-American answer for this, just as there is no logical answer as to why the Department of the United States Post Office ever issued a stamp to glorify the evil Muslim philosophy. A stamp was issued just ten days before the Twin Towers's destruction. After that terrible terrorist attack, a reasonable American would believe that the stamps were recalled. Ah! Not so, for in October 2002, more stamps to glorify Islam were issued. If you have not seen the stamp, I have included a picture of this stamp that Washington "enemies of the people" issued to glorify the most terrorist anti-Christ organization in modern times.

As you read, you will discover that a schizophrenic dual nature or double standard has a grip on Washington politicians.

2003 March 19, 9:30 PM EST—Officially, the war against Iraq began.

2003 March 23—During the period just before Iraq was invaded, an American Muslim soldier threw two hand grenades into an officer's tent in Kuwait that housed more than a dozen officers. Two officers died in that attack, and many were wounded by shrapnel.

In the above incident, it is a situation that can be compared to hiring a fox to guard the chicken house. Why put Muslims in positions that are strategically important? For the same reason that millions of illegal immigrants from below the Rio Grande have been allowed to illegally enter America. A high percentage of these people are emotional people and have learning disabilities. Legal immigration is the way to go, not stealing a way into America. A halfhearted attempt to halt the flow of illegal immigrants from semideveloped or emotional people that have learning disabilities is a destructive act against the soul of America.

2003 May 12—Arab suicide bombers shot their way into three housing compounds in Riyadh, Arabia, killing more than thirty people. Nine of them were Americans.

2003 June 11—A suicide bomber, Arab Palestinian dressed as a Jewish cleric, boarded a bus in Israel and detonated his bomb, killing sixteen and wounding seventy people. Two Americans were among the fatalities. A forty-seven-year-old computer programmer from Cleveland, Ohio, by the name of Alan Beer was killed, and a New Jersey senator's daughter, Sarri Singer, was injured.

President Bush had nothing to say about the Americans being killed and injured but did say, "Some people in the Middle East do not want peace."

Richard Clark tried to emphasize the threats to America from the Muslim terrorists. None of these warnings about the threat to America was taken seriously because President Bush's focus was not on terrorism. His focus was invading Iraq, the little country that he thought could be easily run over with no American deaths.

2003 October 15—Three more Americans killed by Arab terrorists. In addition to the five Americans that were killed and four wounded by a Hamas-engineered bombing at the Hebrew University in Israel on July 31, 2002, and the three American missionaries that were killed and one wounded in Yemen by a tihrty-year-old Arab by the name of Abed Abdul Razak Kamel and the Arab suicide bombers that shot their way into three housing compounds in Riyadh, Arabia, killing more than thirty people, nine of them Americans, on May 12, 2003. On October 15, 2003, a remote-controlled bomb exploded under a diplomatic convoy in Beit Lahia, west Israel, killing three Americans.

The American government has a double standard in its war against terrorism. "Don't do as I do, but do as I say" stands out as the arrogant example of double standard foreign policy. An example of this double standard can be illustrated by the event that occurred in Yemen. Only days after an unmanned killer CIA plane killed al-Quaeda terrorists in Yemen, the U.S. government criticized Israel for killing terrorist leaders in their own land.

2004 March 11, Thursday morning—Ten explosions aboard Spanish commuter trains kill 191 or 192, injuring 1,700. Not all these terrorists were Arabs. However, the terrorist attacks were in retaliation to Spanish military troops being sent to Iraq. George Bush is a direct cause for the terrible deaths and suffering. Instead of holding to his word, "We will go it alone," he wanted other nations to send their citizens to suffer and die in Iraq. He didn't respect the advice he got when the experts said it would be a quagmire. "Bring 'em on," he said. Yes—bring them on, for thousands of good Americans to be killed and God only knows how many maimed.

Saturday, April 3, at 9:03 AM—Spanish police assaulted an apartment building where the suspected terrorists were located. Three terrorists were in the apartment. They set off explosives that killed one police officer and the three terrorists. The Spanish police have reason to believe that five to eight more suspects escaped.

2004 April 2—Colin Powell admitted to the UN that some of the intelligence that was used as an excuse to get Saddam Hussein was flawed. This is a diplomatic way of saying that rumors and George W. Bush's nonfactual personal opinions were used to "go it alone" to get Saddam Hussein. Even the "go it alone" was a blatant lie.

2005 July 7, London, 8:50 AM BST—Three of four Muslims suicide bombers set off their bombs simultaneously in three subway trains. About an hour later, at 9:47, a double-decker bus bombed by the fourth Muslim terrorist. A total of fifty-two people plus the suicide bombers were killed, with seven hundred injured. There were bodies without arms, some without heads, and bits of bodies in the wreckage. The terrorist attack came in retaliation to England's part in the bombing and invasion of Iraq. George Bush and Tony Blair are directly responsible for the carnage. Muslim retaliation for Christians invading a Muslim nation. Tony Blair thanked the people of London for enduring the catastrophe and said that we would not be intimidated, meaning his stand with George Bush has not changed. Tony Blair didn't say who the "we" was.

It certainly wasn't Parliament members and himself. He meant the common ordinary people of England must endure the hardships.

When cultures clash, the weaker side must change their ways and adapt to the ways of the superior power, or violence will erupt if the weaker side refuses to change. It is an age-old pattern that comes down to the present age: the American Indians and the colonists, the Southern slavery states and the Northern nonslave free enterprise states, Jews and Muslims, and now all that that embodies Christian nations and Muslim nations. Americans would not be involved in conflicts with Muslim nations if the self-styled "Caesars" would not be intent on ruling the world from Washington.

I have lived in three neighborhoods in my life, and I only knew a few of my neighbors. They were of Northern European descent, and their children went to the same schools as my children. However, I never interacted with them except when we collected for the Heart Fund and at school functions. We have lived about eighty years and never had any discord with our neighbors. One thought bothers me: why should I be forced to interact with Muslims, when Muslims have proven to be a drag on Christian and Jewish cultures? The Supreme Court unanimously declared that the United States is a Christian nation. Muslims should have never been allowed to immigrate to America. The First Amendment grants us freedom of religion, NOT freedom of philosophies.

A REVIEW THE ROOT CAUSES THAT GENERATES A MENTAL SEETHE AMONG THE WORLD'S PEOPLE

Every thinking American should remember the Recompense Law for "as ye sow, so shall ye reap" to the "jot and tittle," or as the metaphor is given, "an eye for an eye, a tooth for a tooth." America declared war on the Austro-Hungarian Empire on December 7, 1917, and Japan declared war on America on December 7, 1941. The Vietnam and Korean Wars attracted recompense, and a portion of the recompense came on September 11, 2001.

The Waco massacre sent strong disturbances to the Stegokar (humanities great group mind), the Murrah Building bombing and the derailment of the Sunset Limited would not have happened if there had not been a Waco massacre.

The Spanish train bombing would not have happened if Spanish troops had not been sent to war against a Muslim nation, Iraq.

The British subway and bus bombings would not have occurred if Britain's Tony Blair had joined forces with George Bush to invade Iraq.

CHAPTER FOUR

To all political aficionados that have kept current with the Iraq fiasco, you have probably read the outstanding books by Michael Isikoff, David Corn, and Bob Woodward. You may wonder, what more can be said? There is more to be said that has escaped other researchers, and this additional evidence against President Bush is in this chapter. The extreme offenses in the Iraq fiasco are far greater than the minor offenses in Watergate. The combined evidence is so compelling it has the power to have President Bush impeached.

THE REASONS FOR MAKING WAR ON IRAQ FOLLOWS.

There is ample evidence that proves, when George W. Bush entered office in January 2001, he was already determined to have Saddam Hussein deposed or killed.

On the basis of the overwhelming evidence, legal proceedings should decide if President Bush is guilty of malfeasance.

An independent investigator whose co-investigators are not appointed by the president should be empowered by Congress to determine if malfeasance was committed.

This is necessary for there are numerous acts related to the war against Iraq that have mystery associated with them and need to be resolved.

Several serious questions need to be answered. Did President Bush have a predetermined plan before being sworn in as president to invade Iraq? Did the United States military attack Iraq before Congress gave approval? Was money spent on the war that was not approved by Congress?

It is the utmost importance to determine if lies were used to engage the United States in war with Iraq.

LIES NEEDS MORE LIES TO COVER UP FOR THE OLD LIES.

Although President Bush was clever at making quick responses to adversaries in a debate, he did not have the intellectual depth or was not sufficiently clever enough to advance his get-Hussein plan without having his motives revealed.

WHY IRAQ WAS INVADED IS REVEALED.

The testimony of eight men under sworn testimony can reveal the truth as to why Iraq was invaded. Paul O'Neill, Richard Clark, Hans Blix, David McKay, and David McKay's successor, Charles A. Duelfer, and George Tenet are the seven government men that have revealed George W. Bush's premeditated plan to invade Iraq and have revealed the absence of any weapons of mass destruction. This claim was the original reason that was used to make war on Iraq. The eighth man is a Texan that was hired by then-governor Bush to write a biography of Governor Bush. His name is Mickey Herskowitz.

THE TRUTH ABOUT SADDAM'S WEAPONS OF MASS DESTRUCTION (WMD) IS REVEALED BY THE UN INSPECTOR, HANS BLIX.

In 2003, the United Nations inspector Hans Blix stated that Saddam Hussein did not have any weapons of mass destruction for ten years. Later, David McKay reiterated that Saddam Hussein did not have any weapons of mass destruction.

Their reporting to Congress or the UN is certainly NOT the same as a sworn testimony before a grand jury.

FOR MORE INFORMATION ABOUT WHAT CHARLES DUELFER FOUND IN IRAQ, GO TO GOOGLE AND PLUG IN CHARLES A. DUELFER.

Charles Duelfer was the head of the weapons of mass destruction—hunting Iraq Survey Group.

On October 6, 2004, he presented his detailed report about his findings to Congress. He stated that no weapons of mass destruction were found in Iraq. Furthermore, he stated that Saddam did have some weapons of mass destruction before the Iraq-Kuwait war. However, since 1991, his stockpile of chemical weapons began to deteriorate.

In addition to Paul O'Neill, Richard Clark, Hans Blix, David McKay, Charles A. Duelfer, the former CIA head, George Tenet, recently wrote a book about subterfuge of George W. Bush's vice president, Dick Cheney. In his book he reveals how Dick Cheney ignored the facts from the CIA and that Cheney and his people repeatedly pushed the CIA during meetings to ignore the facts and give Cheney the answers he wanted.

If the testimony of these seven former government men plus Mickey Herskowitz is not enough to have President Bush impeached, constitutional law is dead. In its place will have emerged rule by Bill Clinton's third way, or public opinion and edicts.

INTERVIEWING IRAQ'S SCIENTISTS

After several months of Iraq's occupation, Iraqi scientists were interviewed, and they stated that all their weapons of mass destruction were destroyed after the Gulf War.

It was discovered that an Iraqi scientist did try to make a nerve gas and experimented with its effectiveness in 1990. A very revealing article concerning this was published on the front page of the *WSJ*, July 18, 2003. The ricin experiment failed, the testing was discontinued, the scientist, Shakir al-Akidy, told weapons inspectors about his failed plan, inspectors found documents that proved his confession, and Saddam Hussein heard about the discovery and jailed the scientist.

NO ATOMIC BOMBS ANYWHERE IN IRAQ

Saddam did not have enough time to develop any atomic weapons since Israel bombed the Osirak facility in 1981.

However, Saddam was intent on reviving his chemical superweapons arsenal after the sanctions were over and stability was restored to Iraq. Saddam stated to an interviewer that he wanted powerful weapons to deter Iran, for he knew that Iran had started a superweapons program.

THE EIGHTH MAN EMERGES WITH POWERFUL TESTIMONY

President Bush's "ghostwriter," a Texan by the name of Mickey Herskowitz, is the eighth man. He has revealed further information about President Bush's motives for waging war against Iraq.

A SECRET PLAN COMES OUT IN THE OPEN.

President Bush's own "brazen remarks" and his arrogant attitude expressed to Mickey Herskowitz and later to his press secretary, Ari Fleischer, reveal that he had one plan concerning foreign affairs, and that was to either have Saddam Hussein killed or deposed.

According to my findings about this group of seven important figures in government and the United Nations that has information about G. W. Bush's early plan to depose Saddam Hussein, only Paul O'Neill (excepting Dick Cheney) knew that G. W. Bush had intentions of deposing Saddam Hussein in the very early days of Bush's presidency. This idea was discussed in the first ten days of Bush's presidency. However, no plan was ever suggested by cabinet members. About ten months later, Bush was probably irritated that no plan was presented, and he confided his "get Saddam plan" to his secretary of defense, Donald Rumsfeld.

According to Bob Woodward's research, this is revealed in his book *Plan of Attack* and was discussed on the CBS program *Sixty Minutes*, (A transcript of this interview is available on Google).

On November 21, 2001, after a meeting with the National Security Council, President Bush took Donald Rumsfeld to a private room to discuss making war on Iraq. According to Bob Woodward, President Bush said to Rumsfeld, "What have you got in terms of plans for Iraq? What is the status of the war plan? I want you to get on it. I want you to keep it secret." Woodward also revealed that Donald Rumsfeld then told General Tommy Franks to go ahead with a war plan to invade Iraq.

Another good line for an independent investigation is the claim that General Franks later denied that he was ordered by Donald Rumsfeld to plan a war against Iraq.

Planning a war against a foreign nation, using money not allocated by Congress and using the human, economic, and material resources to carry out the plan, was ILLEGAL. The Constitution does not grant "Caesar exploits."

A LOYAL AMERICAN SERVED AS A CABINET MEMBER.

President Bush's first secretary of the treasury, Paul O'Neill, established himself as a business whiz before being sworn in on January 20, 2001, as the seventy-second secretary of the Treasury of the United States.

He was president of International Paper Company from 1985 to 1987. He then served as CEO and chairman of Alcoa from 1987-1999.

His mark in history was amplified when Ron Suskind, a writer for the *Wall Street Journal*, began working on a book titled *The Price of Loyalty*. Many people were interviewed as Ron Suskind gathered information for his book. One of these people that he interviewed was ex-secretary of the Treasury Paul O'Neill.

As Paul O'Neill's destiny unfolded while serving as secretary of the Treasury, President George Bush fired him after two years of service for disagreeing too often with George Bush's tax cuts. The tax cuts increased the yearly deficits and increased the national debt while bashing the poor and middle class and enhancing the rich.

As history was being made in the White House, Secretary of the Treasury Paul O'Neill had a cabinet post that enabled him to sit in on the discussions at cabinet meetings.

Paul O'Neill's contribution to the history of the United States is the fact that he heard and watched discussions about toppling Saddam Hussein.

PAUL O'NEILL STATED TO RON SUSKIND,

> A war with Iraq was being discussed ten days after the inauguration. The main topic at cabinet meetings was toppling Saddam Hussein, and he put a challenge to his cabinet members saying find a way to do this.

Fortunately for America, no cabinet member ever suggested a plan to "get Saddam." Only after ten months in office did President Bush take the plan in his own hands and order Donald Rumsfeld to prepare to "get Saddam."

ANOTHER LOYAL AMERICAN SERVED IN THE BUSH ADMINISTRATION

Richard A. Clarke, whose history in government service has been with National Security and counterterrorism for over ten years, revealed that terrorism was given less priority over the craving to get Saddam. These two prominent Americans give different views that prove that George W. Bush gave less attention to terrorism and craved to get Saddam.

In the months leading up to 9/11, there were one hundred meetings with the national security leadership, yet only two of the meeting were focused on terrorism. Ousting Saddam Hussein—dead or alive—was a private obsession with President G. W. Bush.

By using Dick Cheney's idea to claim that Saddam Hussein had weapons of mass destruction, using unfounded reports, rumors, and opinions unsupported by facts that were used to convince Congress for his "get Saddam at any cost" was malfeasance.

In addition, deceiving the American people and being willing to squander their wealth and have good Americans die for his personal ambitions that included glorifying himself is a crime typical of "political gangsters."

REPORTS OF SADDAM'S WEAPONS OF MASS DESTRUCTION WERE FUDGED.

In addition to the seven government men mentioned, it has been claimed by several reputable reporters that intelligence reports about weapons of mass destruction were fudged. Showing deference to the president of the United States is patriotic respect. However, using euphemisms also is deceiving to the American people and can be perceived as a "cover-up" for untruths and fibs of great magnitude are LIES.

IRAQ WAS NOT A MAJOR THREAT TO PEACE IN THE MIDDLE EAST.

It is a true fact that Israel could have completely destroyed Iraq if Saddam Hussein had become a real threat. Israel is surrounded by millions of hostile Muslims and in a preemptive strike had bombed Iraq's nuclear facility at Osirak in 1981. This prevented Saddam from building an atomic bomb, and if Saddam had restarted a nuclear bomb project, Israel would have bombed it again.

In addition, the fact that Saddam's forces were driven from Kuwait in 1991, and sanctions were restricting any further military excursions. It was next to impossible for Saddam to restart a nuclear bomb program.

DIGGING DEEPER FOR FACTS

However, the nationally known authors that wrote about George W. Bush's lies did not mention the name Mickey Herskowitz.

There may be more investigative reporters that wrote about the Bush Administration, and it is highly likely that more writers will write about George W. Bush's fiasco.

Therefore, in addition to Paul O'Neill having information about G. W. Bush's early plan to make war on Iraq, Mickey Herskowitz knew about George W. Bush's plan to make war on Iraq in 1999, while G. W. Bush was still governor of Texas.

I found this journalist and author's name while searching Google for information that would be pertinent to this account of "Why Iraq was invaded."

I invite all to plug in Mickey Herskowitz on the Google search engine.

The one site on Google that I visited for information had five pages of facts about George W. Bush and his father.

Since I will only use some of the information, I entreat all to access this site. It will be satisfying for those interested in getting a deeper perception of the mindset and the ideas that shaped the future president of the United States, Governor George W. Bush.

MICKEY HERSKOWWITZ THE AUTHOR

Mickey Herskowitz has authored more than thirty books about famous Americans, including "ghostwriting" autobiographies about famous American politicians. He was well-known to the Bush family and was at one time invited to Kennebunkport, Maine, where senior Bush has a vacation home for his family.

While governor of Texas, G. W. Bush selected Mickey Herskowitz to "ghostwrite" an autobiography for him that included a path to the White House, finally titled *A Charge to Keep: My Journey to the White House.*

Herskowitz met with Governor Bush aboutf twenty times to collect data for the autobiography. The profits were to be divided equally in half for Governor Bush and Mickey Herskowitz.

Time passed, and Governor Bush started campaigning for the presidency. At this time, one of G. W. Bush's campaign managers contended with Herskowitz about the record of G. W. in the oil business, and he was told to delete some of the data relative to G. W's oil business. This went against Mickey Herskowitz's principles, and as time passed, one of Bush's campaign people finished the book with flowering credits for G. W's business acumen. Please read it for your information on the Google site.

During these interviews and free discussions, then-governor G. W. Bush revealed some of his private ambitions.

According to the Web page article written by Russ Baker, G. W. Bush revealed his intentions of making war on Iraq in 1999 while he was still governor of Texas. Governor Bush stated:

"To be seen as a great leader, being a great commander-in-chief is a key." He then spoke in a critical way about his father's policies at ending the Iraq-Kuwait war. He then said if he got the chance to invade, he would make political capital and use it to get all the legislation passed that he wanted.

According to Mickey Herskowitz, Governor Bush then stated in an expectant tone that he was going to have a successful presidency.

These are words that come from Mickey Herskowitz. "However, six months later, in 1999, while G. W. Bush was campaigning for the nomination for presidency in New Hampshire, he was asked about Saddam's weapons."

"I'd take them out." Then grinning with a smirk, he continued, "Take out the weapons of mass destruction. I'm surprised he's still there."

Take out the weapons of war of a foreign nation! Not by carrying them out on trucks or another means. Only by an act of war could weapons of war be "taken out" of a foreign nation. However, considering the consequences of war was beyond G. W. Bush's ability. Evidence of this is clear, for G. W. Bush told evangelist Pat Robertson that an invasion of Iraq would be without causalities.

DICK CHENEY WIELDED POWER BEHIND THE SCENES

I have deeply suspected that Dick Cheney was a strong influence before George W. Bush was elected president. As time passed, my suspicions became facts.

Assuming the Herskowitz data is true, it corroborates my early suspicions about George W. Bush and Dick Cheney. Herskowitz recalls that G. W.'s beliefs were based partly on an idea that dates back to the Reagan years. Under Reagan, Dick Cheney was chairman of the House Republican Policy Committee. It was Cheney's idea how to gain political popularity: "Start a small war. Pick a country where there is justification you can jump on, go ahead and invade." (Quotation from the Google Web page.) Granada and Panama were two countries under the Reagan Administration that fitted Cheney's idea.

I RECOMMEND TO ALL INTERESTED IN TRUTH, BUY THE BOOK *HUBRIS* BY ISIKOFF AND CORN.

Two more instances that strongly suggest President G. W. Bush's premeditated attack on Iraq were reported in Isikoff's and Corn's book, *Hubris*. On page 29 in *Hubris*, the authors reveal that before the war against Iraq officially commenced, Rove entered the Oval Office to inform the President about recent polls. He said, "The public isn't buying it." Bush became boisterous and irate. They reported that Bush exploded, saying, "Don't tell me about the fuc—polls. I don't care what the polls say."

Of course he did not care what the polls said. He had a determined premeditated plan and would not be swayed by the thoughts of others.

From page three in the book *Hubris*.

> On May 1, 2002, that was a little more than ten months before the war against Iraq officially began, at a White House briefing, the (now deceased) well-known correspondent, Helen Thomas, was questioning Press Secretary Ari Fleischer about the motives for a war against Iraq. Her questions were not honored honestly and Helen's challenge to the Bush Administration was later conveyed to President Bush. He reacted to this report what seemed to be—enraged—he released a string of expletives. He then responded to his Press Secretary saying, "Did you tell her I don't like mother fuc—that gas their own people? Did you tell her I don't like assholes who lie to the world? "Did you tell her I'm going to kick his sorry motherfuc—ass all over the Mideast?"
>
> Come now, George. Simmer down, little boy. Your outbursts in the White House and the secret cravings to depose Saddam Hussein as told to Mickey Herskowitz are enough to have you removed from office for malfeasance.

GEORGE BUSH DOESN'T LIKE MALACIOUS CONDUCT!

I am near my eightieth year, and through life I have met people that I didn't like. I never liked people that were willing to have people under their command used or killed to advance themselves in some way. I never liked people that tell blatant LIES. I don't like boisterous people that bully and beat others for their own demented reasons. I don't like political leaders that take from the poor and middle class to give it to the rich. I don't like political leaders that increase the public debt that causes the poor and middle class to work longer just to pay interest on the debt. I don't like arrogant people that never accomplished anything on their own and are willing to use "bully tactics" to abuse others for the purpose of advancing themselves. I don't like political leaders that attack a foreign nation without the approval of Congress. I don't like political leaders that take money from one fund and use it to conduct war on a foreign nation without having the funds approved by Congress. I don't like a politician that uses their power to prevent hydrogen from replacing fossil fuels.

I am sure that I have plenty of company as far as choosing what I like and dislike. Most people would not like a political leader that would attack a foreign nation from the position of a self-styled "Caesar."

SELF-STYLED "CAESARS" IGNORE LAWS TO ENGAGE IN FOREIGN WARS.

A "Caesar" exploit was the focus of an article by Roget Loeb that appeared in the *San Francisco Chronicle* on Sunday, June 19, 2005. According to his article, in September 2002, about a hundred American and British warplanes flew from Kuwait, dropped smart bombs on Iraq's air-defense systems, radar detection systems, command and control centers, and communication centers. That was one month before the Congressional vote of approval and two months before the UN resolution 1441 that demanded Iraq to open to unimpeded inspections.

An independent investigator would have ample testimony from subpoenaed witnesses to determine IF George W. Bush committed malfeasance from his predetermined plan to invade Iraq, then using false claims saying Saddam had weapons of mass destruction, he tried to buy yellow cake from Niger, he was in league with Osama bin Laden, and bombed Iraq from a position of a self styled "Caesar" before Congress gave approval.

ATTEMPTS WERE MADE TO ASSASSINATE SADDAM HUSSEIN.

American forces tried repeatedly to kill Saddam Hussein, but when a zealot Muslim by the name of Farouk Hijaza was reported to have engineered a plot to try to kill the first George Bush as he visited Kuwait in April 14-16, 1993, the blame for the assassination attempt was placed directly on Saddam Hussein without evidence.

Washington "Caesars" tried to have Castro assassinated but gave up on the idea when JFK was assassinated. However, that was not an isolated incident. A special training center was created at Camp Benning, Georgia, to train assassins to kill certain Central American and South American politicians. Manuel Noriega (the Panama drug dealer) was trained at this assassin center, and the three El Salvadorian army officers that raped and killed a nun in 1980 were trained at Camp Benning.

Of course, the "political gangsters" in Washington never figured that something thrown out would come back as a boomerang. "Tooth for tooth" is beyond their comprehension. Getting drunk, playing with little boys, having sex with their secretaries, structuring the tax system to make it difficult on the poor and middle class while favoring the rich, and playing "Caesar" on a world scale has been the style of many Washington politicians.

WATCH WHERE YOU STEP WHEN WILD ANIMALS ARE LURKING

More than one person was involved in the assassination attempt of George Bush Senior. Kuwaiti officials interrogated several suspects. It was reported that some of the suspects confessed (or said what the interrogators wanted to hear rather than be tortured) that the Iraqi Intelligence Service was behind the assassination attempt.

That could lead directly to Saddam Hussein. However, many Iraqis were angry with the senior George Bush for the losses the Iraq military suffered during the Desert Storm operation.

It would have been a bold plan for Saddam Hussein to order a president of the United States to be assassinated. However, it was done before when the mafia hired an assassin to kill President John F. Kennedy.

GETTING TO THE BARE FACTS

In April and May of 1993, CIA and FBI technicians went to Kuwait to study the bomb device. They concluded the device was the same as other bomb devices that were used in the Middle East.

Just as American politicians blamed Spain for sinking the battleship *Maine* and declared war on Spain when actually an exploding boiler sank the battleship, they now blamed Saddam Hussein for the assassination attempt.

TRIGGER-HAPPY PEOPLE HAVE MADE WASHINGTON THEIR HOME

In addition, Washington politicians under Reagan blamed Gaddafi for the German discotheque bombing. In response, using no intelligence support, Reagan ordered Libya to be bombed. That wrongful bombing killed Gaddafi's daughter. RETALIATION—"AN EYE FOR AN EYE."

In April 1986, the airline flight number 103 was blown out of the sky by a planted bomb in it luggage compartment. That flight crashed in Lockerbie, Scotland, killing 259 on the plane and eleven on the ground. This terrible terrorist act can be directly traced to Reagan and the bombing of Libya which killed Gaddafi's daughter, just as the Murrah Building bombing and the sabotage of the Sunset Limited can be traced to the Waco massacre.

Later in November 2001, a German court found four with Syrian connections guilty of the 1986 German disco bombing, but the judge stated that the charge that Gaddafi ordered the bombing was NOT proven.

SADDAM COULD HAVE BEEN RESTRAINED BY CONTINUAL SANCTIONS.

Almost everyone considered Saddam Hussein to be a mentally deranged "war-crazed despot," as were Hitler, Stalin, and Mao. (However, for the last 1,500 years, the Muslims have been fighting among themselves.) Yet Saddam's mental affliction can be compared to the "insanity of the Vandals." He had no compunction about ordering the use of gas against his Muslim brothers, ordering the oil wells in Kuwait to be set afire, ordering the valves to be opened and allowing pure crude to empty into the Persian Gulf. These were scandalous acts intent on wanton destruction with no military or political gain.

IN THE SEARCH FOR FAIRNESS AND HONESTY

Since Saddam's regime killed Kurds in northern Iraq and killed thousands of Iranians in the Iran-Iraq War and torture was a routine practice, then, by comparison, what blame is to be imputed to Harry Truman since his intervention in Asians affairs had over one and a half million Vietnamese, Koreans, and Chinese killed plus almost 90,000 Americans killed and frozen to death, and for what? Vietnam DID become a free nation, even with the terrible destruction wrought to their country in the effort to prevent them from becoming free from France. Through American intervention in Korean political affairs, a monster nation has emerged. These wars set the precedents for following "trigger-happy" self-styled "Caesars" to make war on foreign nations.

GEORGE BUSH-CREATED PESTILENCES ENGULF IRAQ

The George W. Bush Iraq war caused one and a half million Iraqis to become refugees in neighboring countries, malnutrition in children to increase to 7.7 percent from 4 percent, infant survival ranking fell to the world's lowest, and schools emphasize teaching the Koran so that in a generation, Iraq will become a fundamentalist Muslim nation. Another statistic that will weigh heavy on the recompense to the United States is the fact that warfare against Muslims and sectarian violence has resulted so far in over 150,000 Iraqis having been killed.

On September 22, 2006, an article in the *WSJ* stated: "In Iraq, torture is greater from sectarian violence than it was during the Hussein regime."

WE WILL GO IT ALONE

When President Bush could not get the United Nations to join in his plan to invade Iraq, President Bush stated, "We will go it alone." In truth, the burden for his "go it alone" plan would be a tremendous sacrifice for good Americans, and a greater financial instability would be created in the American economy.

Since the "free coinage" was illegally stolen from the American people in 1913, twenty-four bond sellers and bondholders skim a profit from every new dollar created, and Americans work longer and longer just to pay interest on illegally created debt. The burden is becoming so great that a financial panic can topple the system that created the outstanding federal notes. If China tries to redeem the American Treasury Notes in 2013, they will not be honored, and a world panic will ensue. If George W. Bush had not craved to "get Saddam" and the debt had been reduced, calamity might have been avoided.

Duping Americans to experience extreme hardship for the insidious motives of self-styled "Caesars" has proven to be easy. It will not last. Americans will eventually wise up. If not sooner, for sure during the reorganization, in the year 2013.

When the Americans being killed in the Iraq fiasco increased and with the cost escalating, President Bush could not comprehend the damage that would be created by excessive debt. He went to the United Nations in the last week of September of 2003 and diplomatically begged the United Nations to share the cost and to send their people to be killed in Iraq.

That was a reverse from "we will go it alone" to "we want other nations to be dying interlopers in Iraq." This makes President Bush a LIAR.

HE TRIED TO KILL MY DAD.

In the case of seeking public support for his craving to make war on Iraq, George W. Bush stated in a speech given in Houston on September 26, 2002, "After all, this is a guy that tried to kill my dad at one time."

Later, when the House Majority leader Dick Armey heard about this remark, he said he just cringed. He then said to his wife, "I hope that's not what this is all about."

Dick Armey, along with all the members of Congress, did not know about Mickey Herskowitz's interviews with George W. Bush in 1999 when G. W. Bush was governor of Texas and remarked to Herskowitz that becoming president and invading Iraq was in his plans.

The cost in dollars from the Bush fiasco just to stay in Iraq is over one billion dollars a week. Already, the Bush administration has increased the federal deficit to the degree that the effects of it will reduce the standard of living for the middle class and expand the debt bubble, so when it bursts in 2013, a great calamity to the American people will result.

It has been said that "pride goeth before a fall." However, stupidity and arrogance of a political leader can cause mortal wounds to the soul of a nation.

THE GREAT CAESAR SAID, "AMERICA IS A WARRIOR NATION."

When the media reported that President Bush actually stated, "America is a warrior nation," it revealed his perception of himself as a modern-day "Caesar."

In 2003, while Liberia was experiencing a civil war, George Bush sent high-ranking Americans to that nation suffering from internal discord to try to quell the discord. It was a moral response to a suffering nation, but a message he had for the Liberian people was astounding. George Bush said that he wanted the people of Liberia to know that America is not just a warrior nation. The fact that a president of the United States admitted publicly that AMERICA IS A WARRIOR NATION should be recorded by historians, and when internal chaos erupts in 2013, the follies of the self-styled "Caesars" will be carefully reviewed.

Publicly admitting that Washington policies have created modern-day "Caesars" is a criminal offense against the American people. To enable this "political gangster" method to enable huge corporations and multibillionaire banking interests to reap financial windfalls from America's interloping into the affairs of foreign nations by printing new money to finance Caesar exploits has been and is the method used to finance their "political gangster" crimes.

PEACE HIJACKED BY WARMONGERS

The fact that America has been cast into the role of a WARRIOR NATION or hijacked by self-styled "Caesars" will come back to bite the American people through the Law of Recompense.

The facts are clear. The abuse to middle-class Americans since 1948 has steadily increased, but no president had the demented gall to publicly admit the fact. Since George W. Bush became president, middle class Americans have been and are being BUSH WHACKED.

THE TENTACLES OF EVIL ARE CRUSHING AMERICA'S ECONOMIC SYSTEM

There are many Americans that are aware of the Washington abuses to the nation and especially the middle class, yet I am not aware of a single comment by news reporters about President Bush's statements concerning the unemployment and dangerous deficit spending that he made in August 2003.

While on a tour, he said that he is interested in making jobs, and when queried about the vast federal debt and the great deficit since he took office, he said, "I am not concerned with figures on a piece of paper. The trust fund is just an empty IOU, just a piece of paper."

NOT CONCERNED WITH FIGURES ON A PIECE OF PAPER?

When I saw him say that on a TV news program, I realized that President Bush's understanding of WHY Americans have to work longer before retirement and work six months a year just to pay taxes is either on par with a LITTLE BOY, or like his father, he really is trying to create havoc with the American financial system to favor the Trilateral Commission and the Bilderberg Club.

Either he has no comprehension of the massive debt bubble that he is helping to expand, or he is eager to create financial instability to help create a WORLD GOVERNMENT that further degrades the standard of living for the vast middle and lower class in America.

A horrible government financial situation is being created that is at par with ENRON'S "cooking the books" debacle. Although those that created the ENRON debacle could be tried in a court, presidents and congressmen can destroy with impunity until the people establish a method to make them responsible. Time is passing, and "as ye sow, so shall ye reap" will be abundantly clear in 2013.

President Bush stated that he is interested in creating jobs while factories are closing due to Washington's policy of exporting manufacturing jobs to foreign nations. The nonmanufacturing or support jobs that he is trying to create and are being created are jobs of a service economy where a high percentage of the jobs are available in warehouses, trucking freight from imported products, keeping records, working in fast-food restaurants, and being employed part-time by Wal-Mart.

OUTSOURCING TO FOREIGN NATIONS HAS UNWANTED EFFECTS

As the twenty-first century opens, even service jobs are being outsourced as the American standard of living declines. Computer programmers, call centers, and centers for keeping records are being outsourced to foreign nations as the "debt bubble" balloons to a condition where catastrophic consequences will result in 2013.

DENYING FEDERAL EMPLOYEES A WAGE INCREASE

In a speech on September 7, 2003, President Bush stated, after further reducing the standard of living to the middle class by his plan to take money from federal employees to finance the Iraq war, that the cost of the Iraq war will be met no matter what the cost. Oh yes, "no matter what the cost" to the poor and the middle class.

After President Bush stated his plan to deny a pay increase to federal employees, Congress again voted themselves a pay raise. The new round of bashing the middle class and enhancing the patricians was revealed with no empathy to the vast middle class. It is time to end being ruled by "political gangsters."

ROGUE NATIONS

The real truth IS that Iran AND North Korea are the nations to recognize as a destabilizing power to world peace, NOT IRAQ.

The American CIA knows that Iran (*WSJ*—05/16/03) has a secret program to produce chemical weapons of mass destruction that can be loaded in the heads of bombs and artillery shells. Bacteria that are the scourges of mankind have been cultured and are ready to use. These terrible disease-causing bacteria being produced in Iran are cholera, smallpox, typhus, and anthrax. The Central Intelligence Agency revealed in an unclassified report that Iran has stockpiled blistering and choking chemicals. In addition to producing chemical and biological weapons, they are concentrating their efforts in producing nuclear weapons. Iran's secret weapons of mass destruction programs began in 1985 during the Iraq-Iran War in response to Iraq's use of chemical and biological weapons against Iran.

Iran's program to make nuclear weapons is now out in the open. It is strategically important for America and the industrialized world to switch to hydrogen as an energy source as quickly as possible. This revelation in this book comes at a very critical time.

IRAN'S PROGRAM TO MAKE WMD IS HEADED BY A WOMAN

An Iranian woman by the name of Samsani was appointed the chief scientist in Iran's program of developing more weapons of mass destruction. She stated that Iran now has about 3,000 scientific researchers, and within a few years, this number is to increase to about 11,000.

It doesn't seem possible, for educating that many Iran students in universities in Germany, England, France, and America in a few years is doubtful.

However, she claimed that Iran was getting technical assistance and equipment from North Korea, China, India, and Russia. Later, it was discovered that Dr. Khan of Pakistan (the brain behind their atomic bomb) was also lending assistance to Iran. The new lethal IEDs (Improvised Explosive Devices) that are being used in Iraq to kill Americans are known to be made in Iran. Since Iran is a Shiite Muslim nation, a bacteria—or gas-laden IED could kill thousands of Americans and Sunni Muslims from one explosive. A radical Muslim has already made a prophecy over the Internet. He stated that Bush's plan to send more Americans to Iraq and stay longer would be met by more Americans being killed. If a suicide bomber or an IED is armed with bacteria or gas, his prophecy will come true.

THE CIA AND THE PENTAGON HAVE GATHERED IMPORTANT INFORMATION ABOUT NATIONS THAT ARE POTENTIAL THREATS TO AMERICA.

One specific report about terrorists meeting in northern Iraq has disappeared from news broadcasts. The Pentagon had a GPS location of some of al-Quaeda's top leaders and wanted to send in cruise missiles, but three times President Bush vetoed the idea in favor of gearing up to get Saddam.

AMERICANS SHOULD DEMAND TO KNOW TRUTH.

George Bush tried to create a psychological smoke screen to take the focus off of his lies. President Bush announced a twelve-billion-dollar plan to put men on the moon and men on Mars. Both ideas are possible, IF a nation is successful at deceiving the public as to WHO is going to finance the project. Twelve billion is a deceiving figure, for many times twelve would be needed to accomplish such an ambitious plan.

A MILITARY STRATEGIST SPEAKS AT THE CARLISLE WAR COLLEGE AGAINST THE IRAQ WAR

During the first weeks of January 2004, a distinguished defense specialist stated in a lecture at the Carlisle War College, "The invasion of Iraq was a strategic error."

He also foresaw the gigantic political problem that would arise from the friction of Sunnis, Shiites, and Kurds. While he did not speculate about the time period needed to unify or separate the contentious Muslim sects, he made it clear that the three Muslim sects are not the only condition that threatens stability. Another strong possibility is the threat of an armed coup taking over the government. This will be present in Iraq as long as contentious Muslim sects have money to buy implements of war.

MILITARY INTERVENTION INTO A FOREIGN NATION WITHOUT DECLARING WAR IS GOING INTO A QUAGMIRE

American troops are still in Korea after fifty years, fortunately none in Vietnam, but a Bush-created quagmire will continue to drain American resources until the "debt bubble" bursts in 2013 or until we have a "balanced budget amendment," and a new political party arises that will represent the interests of the American vast middle class.

George W. Bush was easily able to get support from Tony Blair, the head of a once-great empire, to make war on Iraq. Tony Blair was eager to be a player in world affairs as Great Britain was in the eighteenth and nineteenth centuries. Ego was at stake, and craving to be a player with the most powerful nation on the earth was an egotistical reward. Tony Blair minimized the lack of actual intelligence and maximized the opinions that made the war seem justified. A little fish in gigantic pond craved to be seen as a big fish.

When the North Sea crude is fully exploited, and hydrogen supplants petroleum as the world's energy source, the cash flow from exporting petroleum will cease. Then needy Britons will be reflecting on the big mistake of Tony Blair's Iraq fiasco.

THOSE THAT REVEAL TRUTH RISK BEING PUNISHED.

Even the Pentagon believed that President Bush was openly deceiving—that is, LYING to—the American public and to the world when he claimed that Saddam Hussein had weapons of mass destruction. However, the generals in the Pentagon must be coy about their revelations, for they are prevented from bluntly telling the truth.

A WAR ACE WAS FORCED TO RETIRE

After Bill Clinton was sworn in for his first term, Major General Campbell stated at a speech in Europe that the new "commander in chief" was a draft-dodging, pot-smoking womanizer. The decorated combat pilot was fined about 7,000 dollars and was forced to retire after that statement. However, in his overview analysis, he did not have the slightest idea as to the extent and depth of Bill Clinton's depravity, such as talking about bombing Bosnia with a senator while his female aide was on her knees committing oral sex to the draft-dodging, pot-smoking, womanizing immoral reprobate that tried to establish a SODOM and GOMORRA sociocultural system in the armed services. So for the same reasons, the Pentagon generals could not tell the American public the truth about President George W. Bush.

However, past records prove that Washington politicians lie, cheat, steal, serve themselves most highly, and use government powers to cover up their black deeds.

At times, some info is leaked to persistent reporters. A reporter of the Knight Ridder Newspapers can illustrate a good example of ethics by media people. On June 7, 2003—that was eighty-one days after the official attack on Iraq, Knight Ridder published the following article. It is not a complete quote for respect to copyrights. However, quotation marks do indicate a direct quote. The following is the essence of the article.

The Pentagon doubts claims of WMD.

No evidence was found by intelligence officers to prove that Iraq was producing WMD.

Washington—A review of intelligence documents and the testimony of current and former intelligence officials reveal that President Bush and his top aides used unverified claims to make a convincing story to support his war on Iraq. Claims that Saddam Hussein was a real threat were actually exaggerated stories from what American spies knew.

Bush and his aides presented White House spin or stories about the threat posed by Saddam Hussein as truth. Stories that came from the White House for convincing the public and Congress that Saddam had ties to terrorists and had a nuclear weapons program were either false or debatable.

President Bush, Secretary of Defense Donald Rumsfeld, and Secretary of State Colin Powell claimed that Saddam Hussein was actually producing and stockpiling biological and chemical weapons.

However, on Friday, senior Pentagon officials confirmed significant doubts were presented in a classified report titled: Iraq—"Key Weapons Facilities—An operational Support Study."

This intelligence report gave a counterclaim to Bush's reason for going to war.

Six months before the war officially began, the Pentagon's Defense Intelligence Agency had gathered intelligence that did not support the White House's claims that Saddam was a threat and was producing or had WMD.

A portion of the Pentagon's report was very definitive. It stated, "There is no reliable information on whether Iraq is producing and stockpiling chemical weapons, or whether Iraq has—or will—establish its chemical warfare agent production facilities."

The report acknowledged that Saddam once had biological weapons stockpiles. However, uncertainty prevails regarding if Saddam still had any stockpiles prior to Iraq being attacked. The amount is unknown.

The Defense Intelligence Agency's report and growing knowledge about Saddam Hussein's war machine fueled a debate about White House pressure on CIA analysts to alter intelligence estimates to favor Bush's reason for making war on Iraq.

The Defense Intelligence Agency's report was finished at a time when President Bush was launching a public relations effort to gain support for making war on Iraq. He was still claiming that Saddam Hussein was in league with terrorists and had weapons of mass destruction.

There are about sixteen more paragraphs that are focused on President Bush's efforts to have doctored intelligence reports used to convince Congress and the American public in his zeal to depose or kill Saddam Hussein.

A SENATE INTELLIGENCE COMMITTEE'S REPORT AGREED WITH THE KNIGHT RIDDER ARTICLE.

On July 9, 2004, one year and one month after the article appeared in the Knight Ridder publication, the Senate Intelligence Committee blasted the government's own intelligence agencies for unfounded assumptions instead of solid evidence in claiming weapons of mass destruction existed in Iraq. The intelligence committee reported that conclusions were exaggerated or were simply opinions.

Blasting the government's own intelligence agencies means blaming the executive branch, and that means blaming President Bush.

President Bush's forceful claiming that Saddam Hussein was in league with Osama bin Laden, Saddam tried to buy raw fission material (yellow cake) from Niger, and Saddam had weapons of mass destruction had become discredited. President Bush then switched his claim for the Iraq war to defeating terrorism. His speeches began to use "to defeat terrorism" for the reason for the Iraq war. When possible, while speaking to an audience, each time the word "terrorism" was spoken, it was spoken with emphasis while he paused for a moment and scanned the audience from right to left.

However, he never clearly defined or presented proof that world terrorism had roots in Iraq. He relied on the American people's great resentment for the 9/11 attacks to manipulate public opinion to support his personal goals.

If President Bush meant the sectarian violence in Iraq to be classified as terrorism, then the only solution to sectarian violence would be to partition all three Muslim sects. This could not happen, for the Sunnis would be "cut out" of any land rich in oil. He did not offer any solution to end the sectarian violence.

If President Bush meant the insurgency against Americans was terrorism, he was fantasizing, for Americans from a Christian nation invading a Muslim nation will guarantee a continual and expansion of guerilla war against the interlopers into Muslim affairs. Leaders of Iran have recently stated: Peace will not come to Iraq as long as Americans are present.

I repeat: Since President Bush's claims have changed his reason for war with Iraq from having WMD to trying to establish democracy, would he honor a referendum vote by the Iraqi people? A simple question on a referendum ballot would suffice. It could simply ask: Do you want the Americans to stay or GO? Would George W. Bush honor the democratic vote? The answer is of course not. He wants to be a self-styled "Caesar" and rule the world from Washington.

EX-PRESIDENTS JIMMY CARTER AND GERALD FORD PLUS EX SECRETARY OF STATE HENRY KISSINGER DISSAPROVED OF THE IRAQ WAR.

In an interview with *Washington Post's* Bob Woodward in July 2004, ex-president Gerald Ford stated he "very strongly" disagreed with President Bush's reasons for invading Iraq.

In July 2005, ex-president Jimmy Carter stated, "I thought then, and I think now, that the invasion of Iraq was unnecessary and unjust. And I think the premises on which it was launched were false."

On May 19, 2007, during a prepping to sell his latest literary work, President Carter again focused on the George W. Bush's administration, in response during an interview, saying, "I think as far as the adverse impact on the nation around the world, this administration has been the worst in history."

On Sunday, November 19, 2006, ex-secretary of state Henry Kissinger stated on a TV interview that he no longer believed a military victory in Iraq was possible. He also stated that he didn't believe sectarian violence could be controlled. Of course, he was claiming that the U.S. military couldn't control sectarian violence.

It is a repeat of the wise analysis of Henry Kissinger and Robert McNamara when they said the Vietnam War was wrong, a political and military mistake.

BILLIONS OF DOLLARS WILL BE NEEDED TO REBUILD THE DAMAGE FROM THE DESTRUCTION OF IRAQ.

Under the direction of President George W. Bush, the destruction in Iraq has reached the extent of vying with the Vietnam fiasco. Terrible human suffering and deaths and billions of dollars of American money wasted will scar the American soul, and America's economic condition will be destabilized when the calamity in 2013 occurs.

MIDTERM ELECTIONS OF 2006

Democratic politicians in Congress should know the American people did not vote for Democrats in the midterm elections, they voted against Republicans.

However, on the plus side, Democrats will be more inclined to create a hydrogen industry and put into operation the offer of my Social Security plan.

Assuming the Democratic Congress will create a hydrogen industry with a new Social Security plan, it will be joined with the first two great blessings to the American nation. The first being Roosevelt's Social Security plan, the second being Eisenhower's interstate highway system.

A National Hydrogen Industry could be the third great blessing, with profits going into a Social Security fund. If established, it will be unprecedented in world history. The effects would improve the world and enable greater wealth for 90 percent of all Americans. However, the restructuring that will come in 2013 is inevitable.

IF the Democrats try to advance a SODOM and GOMORRAH sociocultural system, since they have now gained control of Congress, they will be stigmatized as a party of sexual perverts. If this becomes true, their popularity will wane, and the political process may require a new political party to save America from further decay and financial ruin.

Remember, readers, it will be reaping time in 2013 for the follies of not balancing the budget, creating a destructive financial condition from huge debt, and interfering with the internal affairs of foreign nations are going to cause chaos.

HELPING THOSE IN NEED IS MORALLY RIGHT. STEPPING IN AND DOING THEIR WORK FOR THEM IS MORALLY WRONG

It is incumbent upon the developed people to aid those striving to develop. However, usurping their sovereignty by using force to do their work for them is against God's development plan for humanity.

When America had race riots, it would have been absolutely wrong for China or Russia to send military forces into our country to solve our social or political problems.

Galatians 6:5, KJV, "For every man shall bear his own burden."

Every nation shall bear their own burdens. Interloping in the affairs of foreign nations as America did with Vietnam, Korea, Somalia, and Iraq interferes with the natural development of that nation and is a sin against God and therefore a sin against humanity.

Harry Truman's war acts against Vietnam and Korea were morally wrong and unconstitutional.

America did not lose the war with Vietnam and Korea. American leaders chose a wise strategic withdrawal rather than use all the resources at our command and commit genocide and almost complete destruction to those small Asian nations.

The same is true for Iraq. It was morally wrong and unconstitutional to invade Iraq. Only by committing genocide and complete destruction can a war victory be realized.

For humanitarian reasons, continual killing and destruction must cease. A humanitarian withdraw is the only choice.

FOR INDIVIDUALS, FOR GROUPS, AND NATIONS:

"As ye sow, so shall ye reap."

George Bush: you should have listened to Lawrence Lindsey and General Shinseki, you should have worked for peace not war.

Now your future is dark. You have also created a dark future for your associates.

www.ingramcontent.com/pod-product-compliance
Lightning Source LLC
Chambersburg PA
CBHW031251280526
45784CB00004B/1811